TO CIVIL WAR

Kansas-Missouri, 1854–61

llier-Macmillan Limited, London

For James M. Mundis
who in many ways never left Kansas

Library of Congress Catalog Card Number: 71–92071

The Macmillan Company
Collier-Macmillan Canada Ltd., Toronto, Ontario

Printed in the United States of America

FIRST PRINTING

Title page illustration courtesy of Kansas State Historical Society

CONTENTS

C.2

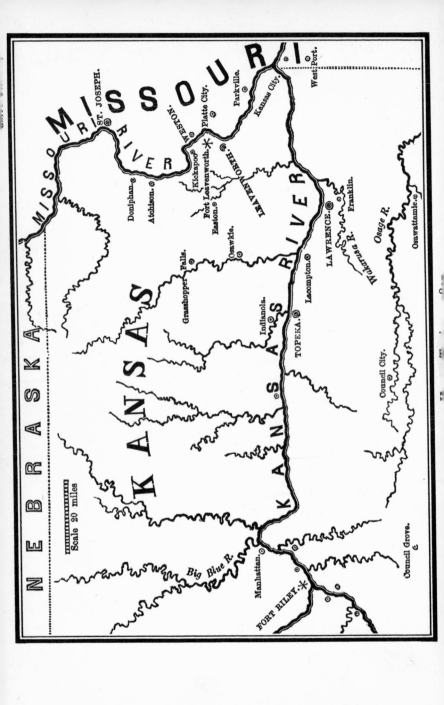

A NOTE TO
THE READER

Numerous personalities appear and reappear during this examination of the Kansas-Missouri border wars. A list of some of the more important names is below, as well as a list of the territory's governors and the dates of their tenures. And, so the possible bias of certain reports can be evaluated, a list of the territorial newspapers and an indication of their partisanship is also included.

Protagonists & Antagonists

ATCHISON, DAVID R.—Ardently Proslavery senator from Missouri (in the later stages of the conflict, ex-senator) who led border armies into the territory several times.

BRANSON, JACOB—A Free Soil man with whom the murdered Charles Dow had lived. Captain of a band of Kansas Regulators, he was captured by Proslavery forces, then rescued by Free Soilers, an act which precipitated the Wakarusa War.

BUFORD, JEFFERSON—An Alabaman who sold his slaves, used the money to raise a private army and then led his men to the territory to support the Proslavery side.

CLARKE, GEORGE W.—One-time Indian agent, a leader of the Proslavery forces.

DOY, DR. JOHN—A Free Soiler who tried to escort free Negroes from the territory and was arrested by Missourians for slave-stealing.

DOW, CHARLES—A Free Soiler murdered by a Proslavery man over a disputed piece of wooded land.

HAMILTON, CHARLES A.—A young Georgia emigrant who captained the Proslavery forces in southern Kansas and was responsible for the Marais des Cygnes massacre.

HARVEY, JAMES A.—A Chicagoan who deserted his wife and daughter in quest of adventure in Kansas. He was one of the more active Free Soilers and led a group sometimes known as Harvey's Forty Thieves.

JACKSON, ZACHABOD—Proslavery commander who brought a group of Georgia volunteers into Kansas.

JACKSON, CLAIBORNE C.—Border Ruffian.

JONES, SAMUEL—A native Missourian who was elected sheriff of Douglas County, Kansas. He was militantly anti-Free Soil.

LANE, JAMES H.—An ex-congressman from Indiana who came to Kansas seeking to organize the Proslavery Democratic party there. Rejected, he switched to the Free Soil side and became one of its two most important leaders. A mercurial and flashy demagogue of few scruples.

MONTGOMERY, JAMES—Dominant Free Soil leader in southeastern Kansas. A former preacher who became the best known of the Jayhawkers.

PHILLIPS, WILLIAM—Reporter for the *New York Tribune.* Strongly biased in favor of Free Soilers and an active participant in many of their undertakings.

POMEROY, SAMUEL C.—Early settler in the territory and active Free Soil leader.

ROBINSON, DR. CHARLES—Co-leader, with Lane, of the Free Soilers. Agent of the New England Emigrant Aid Society, perhaps *the* most influential man in the Free State party.

STRINGFELLOW, DR. JOHN—Militant Proslavery ex-Missourian who edited the *Squatter Sovereign.*

SUMNER, COLONEL E. V.—Commanding officer of the United States First Cavalry.

TITUS, HENRY—Active Proslavery man whose home was garrisoned and fortified.

WALKER, SAMUEL—Free Soiler who considered himself a close friend of James Lane and who led the attack against Fort Titus. In the latter stages of the conflict he was first sheriff, then deputy marshal.

WHITFIELD, J. W.—Proslavery agitator and territorial delegate to Congress.

WILKES, WARREN D.—South Carolinian who brought a Proslavery force into the territory.

WOOD, SAMUEL—Captain of the Free Soil party that rescued Jacob Branson.

Newspapers

Proslavery: *Kansas Pioneer*
            Leavenworth Herald
            Squatter Sovereign

Free Soil: *Herald of Freedom*
            Kansas Free State
            Kansas Tribune

Governors

Reeder, Andrew H. . . . 1854–55
Shannon, Wilson   . . . 1855–56
Geary, John W.   1856–57
Walker, Robert J. 1857
Denver, James W.   . . . 1858
Medary, Samuel   1858–60

Acting Governors

Woodson, Daniel   . . . . (at intervals) 1855–57
Stanton, Frederick P. . . . (at intervals) 1857
Denver, James W.   1857–58
Walsh, Hugh S.   . . . . (at intervals) 1858–60
Bebe, George M.   . . . . (at intervals) 1860–61

INTRODUCTION

President Franklin Pierce signed the Kansas-Nebraska Act on May 30, 1854. His pen might just as well have been a match, for his signature lit a fuse that burned for seven chaotic and bloody years in the Kansas Territory, then reached the powder keg at its end—which blew the Union apart with civil war.

This war, in which Americans shot, hacked, stabbed and bludgeoned to death 204,000 of their countrymen and lost 400,000 more to sickness and disease (a greater number of fatalities than the United States suffered in World Wars I and II combined) has been assigned a variety of causes. The most common are: industrialism versus agrarianism, biased tariff laws, mercantilism, unfair legislative representation, Yankee oppression and southern treachery.

But the issue was slavery. Nothing more, nothing less. Without this "peculiar institution," the Civil War would never have been fought.

Extremists had held the public ear for nearly half a century. Swaggering with pompous self-righteousness, the North congratulated itself on its high moral standards and never missed a chance to condemn the South. The South on the other hand had become paranoid, saw Yankee plots everywhere and screamed back at its critics with shrill hostility.

Slavery was wrong. Obviously. And there is ample documentation to prove that most people, North and South, knew, or at least at one time had known this.

But the South was caught in a horrible trap very much of its own making. Southern economy was based entirely upon the slave system. Without slaves the South could see nothing but its own collapse. But more important were the great lengths to which the majority of southern whites, their churches and their state legislatures had gone to convince themselves and their slaves that *Negroes were not human.* The black, according to popular belief, was a subspecies that occupied a rung on the evolutionary ladder between monkeys and men.

Many, if not most, southern whites believed this. They had to in order to justify the slave system to themselves.

In 1900, thirty-five years after the end of the Civil War and the alleged granting of equality to blacks, a book was published entitled *The Negro a Beast, or In the Image of God.* Its title page claimed: "The Negro [is] a beast, but created with articulate speech, and hands, that he may be of service to his master—the White man." Chapter 1 is headed: "The Formation of the Negro and other Beasts—then Man on the Sixth Day." This is no simple and easily dismissed hate pamphlet. It is a book whose author "spent fifteen years of his life, and $20,000 in its compilation." It was published by the American Book and Bible House, St. Louis, Missouri.

Brief reflection on the major national events of the last decade will reveal that the idea of the Negro as an animal is still very much alive, if a bit more subtly promoted.

Consider, then, the position of the white Southerner in the 1850s. The fortunes of a slaveholding aristocrat were dependent upon the continued existence of slavery. No one, particularly if he is wealthy, destroys his source of income. And how was this man, who so loudly glorified the American ideals of liberty and freedom, to admit that he had made slaves of his fellow men?

More significant, how could the *poor* white stand it? Living in semipoverty, barely eking a living from a few acres of soil, he comprised the bulk of the South's white population. The Negro gave him a certain status, gave him something to look down on. If the slaves were freed, the poor white could anticipate two very personal and unbearable disasters. First, a horde of manpower would be set loose that could afford to work for even less money than he could. Second, he must view himself as socially no more worthy than a slave, than a "field nigger," than an animal. And this beast would then invade his towns, his schools, his churches, even his home, and eventually (what agony to contemplate!) he might even take the white man's woman—as the white man had been taking black women for the last three centuries.

The abolition of slavery was unthinkable, not only to the aristocrat but to the dirt farmer who could never hope to own a slave.

The issue was slavery.

The war began in the Kansas Territory.

1.

THE ACT

The Kansas-Nebraska Act was largely the work of Illinois Senator Stephen A. Douglas. Douglas was an energetic five-footer whose bombastic character caused many of his contemporaries to love, fear or hate him with unrestrained passion. This was the "Little Giant," the oratorical powerhouse with whom Lincoln clashed on the debating platform and whom Lincoln eventually defeated for the Presidency of the United States.

Douglas's motives have been hotly argued by scholars and historians for the last century. His defenders have called him a sterling patriot and a master politician. His critics have condemned him as a stupid opportunist, a coward and an evil man. It is impossible to state the literal, incontestable truth behind his engineering of the bill, but there is sufficient evidence upon which to base a tenable assumption.

First, though, we must look back to 1820. The common practice had been to admit new states to the Union on a "one for you, one for me" basis. Alabama had been accepted in 1819, balancing the scales at eleven slave, eleven free. Now there was a Missouri statehood bill before Congress. Missouri had first petitioned in 1819, as a potential slave state, but the North and the South had not been able to agree and thus Missouri was still a territory.

There was a good deal of antislavery sentiment in the air. An amendment had been tacked to the Missouri bill that forbade the further importation of slaves into the proposed state, and set free at the age of twenty-five all slaves born within her boundaries from the day she was admitted to the Union. It required only minimal insight to realize that this amendment would rid Missouri of slaves within a generation. The South, naturally, rejected the amended bill.

The North kept pressing. It had long been unhappy with the "federal ratio," an arithmetic formula that, in effect, classified a slave as three-fifths of a human being and gave to the South roughly twenty congressional seats and twenty electoral votes on the singular basis of its slave population. The number of seats granted to a state in the House of Representatives was, and still is of course, computed on the basis of that state's population. Southern states were allowed to count the slaves within their boundaries and then add three-fifths of that number to the number of their white population. Congressional seats were apportioned on the basis of the total figure. The North interpreted the potential admission of Missouri, with slave-state status, as an aggressive move by the South to increase its federal voting power.

The South had no intention of surrendering the right

to carry its property wherever it pleased. Quite clearly, the North wished to deprive the South of this fundamental liberty.

The argument dominated the nation's thoughts for nearly two years. Remnants of the fading Federalist party and Jeffersonian Republicans from the middle states saw a chance to unite the North on this issue, strengthen their organizations and snatch the political leadership from the hands of the Virginia aristocracy.

Evidently, more northern politicians were opposed to a renaissance of federalism than to an extension of slavery and they threw their needed votes to the South, which, with the added weight, was now strong enough to get as well as to give.

The Compromise of 1820, or the Missouri Compromise, was the result.

Its essence was this. The territories of Maine (free) and Missouri (slave) were to frame state constitutions. The Missouri document need not contain any restrictions of slavery, but the state would not be allowed to exclude free Negroes and mulattoes (as it originally wished to do). And slavery would henceforth be forbidden from all United States territories north of the 36° 30′ parallel, which was Missouri's southern boundary.

Twelve slave states, twelve free states.

The South could look forward to the admission of Arkansas and Florida as slave states in the near future; and the North had secured for itself the geographically larger area of the unsettled territory west of Illinois.

Neither side was ecstatic, but each felt it had made important gains.

An uneasy peace held sway for the next thirty years. Then, in December 1849, the battle flags were unfurled again. This time California ran them up the poles. She applied for statehood, and the constitution she submitted banned slavery within her boundaries.

California wanted to come in free. The balance was then fifteen states slave and fifteen states free. California would swing the power to the North. The South's immediate reaction was: *No.*

There was an additional, quite important issue here. California was part of the large territory ceded to the United States by Mexico in 1848. Tension had run high over this new land. Would it be slave or free? If both, then in what proportions? Each side wanted to know, each wanted it settled, each wanted the larger slice of the pie.

It seemed quite likely that California would set up a separate and independent government if it were refused admission to the Union with a constitution of its own choice. It was inhabited by 49'ers and others with a taste for adventure. They were people of initiative who, without waiting for congressional sanction, had drafted and approved a constitution by a vote of twelve thousand to eight hundred, had elected a governor and a legislature and were now only waiting for Washington to ratify their actions.

Nobody wanted to see them go their own way.

The North supported California vigorously. The South was resolute in its opposition. It had defeated the Wilmot Proviso in '47—which would have restricted the extension of slavery—and it was determined to maintain this freedom.

President Zachary Taylor, himself a slaveholder and a Louisiana planter, stunned the South by seeing no reason why California should not be admitted with her proposed constitution.

Impasse. Tempers soared.

The elderly John C. Calhoun wrote to his daughter: "I trust we shall persist in our resistance [to California's admission] until the restoration of all our rights, or disunion, one or the other is the consequence. We have borne the wrongs and insults of the North long enough."

The governor and legislature of South Carolina refrained from immediate secession only because they hoped that with additional time more southern states would accompany them. A convention was called in Nashville, Tennessee, to discuss ways to defend southern interests against continuing northern oppression.

Historian Samuel Eliot Morison finds it difficult to determine the reason for all this sound and fury. The South had never suffered any really telling blow at the hands of the North and, in fact, had gotten most of what it wanted. "But there was a positive, almost utopian aspect to secession," Morison writes. "A vision of a great slaveholding republic stretched from the Potomac to the Pacific, governed by gentlemen and affording perfect security to their property in human beings, monopolizing the production of cotton and so dictating to the world, was beginning to lift up the hearts of the younger and more radical Southern leaders."

Compromise was needed.

The Great Compromiser, Senator Henry Clay of Kentucky, set to work. He introduced what was known as the Omnibus Bill, which contained five proposals he hoped would satisfy both sides. They sparked one of the greatest Senate debates of the last century. Clay spoke for two days, persuading the North it could not have its way in total, and pacifying the South, soothing its ruffled feathers. Calhoun demanded that the North must "do justice by conceding to the South an equal right in the acquired territory" and must "cease the agitation on the slave question." Senator William H. Seward of New York, who was later to be attacked in the assassination plot that killed President Lincoln and still later to buy Alaska from Russia, strenuously opposed any capitulation to the South. He referred to that higher, moral law, which he regarded as being unalterably opposed to slavery. But the venerable Daniel Webster supported Clay and it was his great influence that eventually swung the North. Compromise, it seemed, had been reached.

But things were not as they seemed and the compromise was defeated, mostly by President Taylor's refusal to make California's admission dependent upon bribes to the South. He further stated that if any region tried to secede, he would personally lead the federal army to force it back into the Union.

Crisis.

But then Taylor died in office on July 9 and was succeeded by Millard Fillmore, who was in favor of the Compromise. Senator Douglas of Illinois broke the Omnibus Bill into five separate bills and hastily brought them forward. The Senate, after a brief debate, passed them and sent them to the House, which also passed them. Fillmore signed, and the Compromise of 1850 became law.

It contained four highly important provisions: (1)

California would be admitted with its antislave constitution. (2) Slave trade—but not slaveholding—was banned in the District of Columbia. (3) A new and quite stringent law insuring the return of fugitive slaves was passed. (4) The remainder of the Mexican cession was to be organized into two territories, Utah and New Mexico, in which slavery could exist until and unless the settlers decided otherwise in their legislatures.

Item four was crucial. Since Utah lay entirely above the 36° 30′ parallel, the Compromise of 1850 implicitly repealed the doctrine of the Missouri Compromise. It also paved the way for Kansas's Seven Years War— prelude to the Civil War.

Now, in 1854, we come to Stephen A. Douglas and the Kansas-Nebraska Act. There are five major schools of thought concerning Douglas's motivations: (1) He was aspiring to the Presidency. (2) He was paving the way for a centrally routed transcontinental railroad. (3) He desired to remove slavery as an issue from the chambers of Congress. (4) He was seeking personal monetary gain. (5) He wished to open the frontiers for an expanding nation.

Douglas was a driving, ambitious man who had advanced rapidly up the ranks of the Democratic party. But it is clear that high position was not enough for him—he wanted to go to the top. He made a vigorous bid for the presidential nomination in 1852, but lost to Franklin Pierce. Pierce went on to capture the Presidency, then snubbed Douglas by giving him no part or power in the new administration. Douglas did not intend to stay in the background, but to try again required support, strong support. And the backing of southern democrats was essential.

The Senator had a long history of interest in railroads. A member of the Illinois legislature in 1836, he had been instrumental in the building of the Illinois railroads. This strengthened his position with both his constituents and the railroad tycoons.

In 1844, as a member of the House, Douglas responded to Secretary of War William Wilkins's suggestion that the territory west of Missouri be opened, by introducing a bill to organize the Territory of Nebraska. No action was taken.

In 1845, Douglas authored an eight-page pamphlet which argued that the railroads from the East should converge at Chicago, and that the western road should begin at Chicago and proceed from there to the Pacific, "if that country could be annexed in time."

In 1848, Douglas, now a Senator, introduced yet another bill to organize the Nebraska Territory, and again no action was taken.

In 1852 he bought seventy acres in Chicago proper, bringing his combined holdings of Chicago real estate and western lands to thirty-three hundred acres. A transcontinental railway following a central route and having as its hub the city of Chicago would have made Douglas's land holdings quite valuable indeed.

In 1853 the undauntable Senator introduced a third Nebraska bill, which also failed.

Since Douglas's bill of 1848, political and common debate on the subject had been growing ever more intense. Senator David R. Atchison of Missouri crystallized the southern view when he said in 1853 that supporters of the bill "assumed that slavery was excluded from that Territory by the law commonly called the Missouri Compromise. If so, I was then and am now opposed to interfering with that Territory unless that restriction is removed . . . I will support a bill to organize a government for the Territory upon the condition that such bill contains no restriction upon the subject of slavery . . . I now say emphatically that I will not vote for any bill that makes Nebraska a freesoil Territory."

Months later, nine days after the Thirty-third Congress convened, Senator A. C. Dodge of Iowa introduced a new Nebraska bill. It was referred immediately to the Senate Committee on Territories, of which Stephen A. Douglas had long been chairman. Douglas set to work with a vengeance.

It should be pointed out that the Illinois senator was a member of the F Street Mess, a group of politicians— many of them from the South, including Missouri's Senator Atchison, soon to be infamous—who lived together in the same rooming house.

The result was that the huge land area was carved into two territories: Kansas (west of Missouri) which, it was tacitly assumed, would enter the Union as a slave state, and Nebraska (west of Iowa) which was assumed would enter as a free state. The device through which this evasion of the Missouri Compromise was to be accomplished was known as *Popular Sovereignty*. The precedent had been established by the Compromise of 1850, wherein Congress had declined to impose any restriction upon slavery in the territories. The doctrine was simple: The people of any given territory could determine for themselves whether slavery would or would not exist within their jurisdiction. It seemed, in the context of the moment, fair and reasonable. It would shortly prove disastrous.

At first Douglas attempted to have the document worded vaguely, avoiding any specific stand on slavery. Atchison and his compatriots would not settle for this. Douglas reworked it, and the final wording left no room for misinterpretation:

> [The Missouri Compromise] Which, being inconsistent with the principle of non-intervention by Congress with slavery in the States and Territories, as recognized by the legislation of 1850, commonly called the compromise measures, *is hereby declared inoperative and void* [italics mine] it being the true intent and meaning of this act not to legislate slavery into any territory or state, nor to exclude it therefrom; but to leave the people thereof perfectly free to form and regulate their domestic institutions in their own way, subject only to the Constitution of the United States.

This was more to the South's liking. It approved and the bill passed the Senate, then went to the House. There it sustained some minor alterations and returned to the Senate on May 25, 1854. The North made a final effort to block it. But Atchison, Douglas and President Pierce —who sorely needed the support of discordant elements in his party and could not gain it without the powerhouse of Atchison-Douglas influence—managed to swing the vote.

On May 30 President Pierce signed the bill into law.

Senator Archibald Dixon of Kentucky said to Senator Douglas, "Sir, I once recognized you as a demagogue, a mere manager, selfish and intriguing. I now find you a warm-hearted and sterling patriot."

Anticipating the bill's passage, Atchison had been urging Missourians to be ready to rush across the border and claim Kansas for the South. Missouri's border counties alone contained fifty thousand slaves—approximately a $30 million investment. Atchison had written that "to have a free state as our western neighbor would spell disaster."

"If I had my way," cried Dr. John Stringfellow, a rabid proslavery Missourian who was to play a prominent part in the Kansas wars, "I'd hang every damned abolitionist! And everyone north of the Mason-Dixon line is an abolitionist."

Senator Atchison's newspaper, the *Platte Argus,* appealed: "Citizens of the West, South, and Illinois! Stake out your claims and woe be to the Abolitionist or Mormon who shall intrude upon it or come within reach of your long and true rifles, or within point blank shot of your revolvers."

The North mourned and its sentiment found voice in Senator Benjamin F. Wade of Ohio. The day before the passage of the act Wade said, "I believe there is to be an eclipse of the sun and I think that the sun in the heavens and the glory of this republic should both go into obscurity and darkness together. Let the bill pass then. It is a proper occasion for so dark and damning a deed."

But it wasn't long before the North's competitive spirit rose. "Come on then, gentlemen of the slave states!" Senator Seward cried. "Since there is no escaping your challenge, I accept it, in behalf of freedom. We will engage in competition for the virgin soil of Kansas and God give victory to the side that is stronger in numbers as it is in right."

2.

KANSAS IS SLAVE SOIL

Far to the west of Washington, Kansas slept as it had for centuries, in undisturbed tranquility—ignorant that it was now considered the spoils of war, ignorant that it was about to be raped, its soil soon to be stained with blood.

The Kansas Territory was a vast grassland 200 miles long by nearly 700 miles wide, somewhat more than 130,000 square miles of rich virgin soil. The buffalo had fled to the far western reaches, where the Great American Desert lay, and most of the fur-bearing animals had been trapped out years before. But small game still abounded. Lush grass rolled for miles over treeless prairies. There were creeks and streams, bordered by healthy stands of hardwoods and softwoods.

On the day Franklin Pierce signed the Kansas-Nebraska Act there were, excluding the military, less than eight hundred whites living in Kansas.

But there were innumerable Indians: Shawnee, Seneca, Delaware, Pottawatomi, Sac, Fox, Apache, Kiowa,

Oto, Ioway, Missouria, Kickapoo, Kaskaskia, Wea, Peo-
ria, and several other tribes. During the Senate debates,
old Sam Houston of Texas had reminded his colleagues
again and again that these Indians (some of whom were
native, others who had been removed there from the
North and the East) had been guaranteed this land by
treaty for "as long as grass shall grow and water run."

Leaders of the various tribes were summoned to Washington and quickly divested of their lands. Less than a
month after the act had been passed, the government
proudly announced that the Indians had handed over
several millions of rich, fertile acres, which were now
open for settlement.

But the firebrands on both sides were disappointed.
Great waves of men did not wash over the borders to
inundate the Kansas Territory. They trickled in, and
even then with a little reluctance. Newspapers, politicians
and sectional patriots on both sides were whipping up
loud campaigns. "Save Kansas for God and Freedom!"
"Hold Kansas for the South and for your pride!" "Contain the monster of Slavery!" "Stop the evil of Abolition!" And while everyone who could read, or even so
much as listen to an impassioned speech, agreed that yes,
Kansas should be for the North, or that yes, Kansas
should be for the South, few of them were willing to
pull up stakes and go settle this new land that had no
government, that had no towns, that had no stores, that
had little, actually, but grass.

Missouri bordermen made the first sallies. They were
rough, brawling men, most of whom had lived on or
beyond frontiers for much of their lives. Many had

fought in the Mexican War; others had been furtrappers in the Rockies; and there were Indian fighters and buffalo hunters among them. In short, they were men to whom adventure would appeal—an adventure like the taking of Kansas. And Kansas was no farther than a short ferry ride across the Missouri River.

On June 10 a group of them crossed the river, rode to Salt Creek valley, read a hot-tempered proclamation that slavery was hereby instituted in the Kansas Territory, then went back with the satisfaction of a job well done. Later in the summer bordermen managed to found three proslavery towns, Leavenworth, Kickapoo and Atchison, on the west bank of the Missouri. Enough of them remained to make the settlements towns in something more than name, but most returned to their home state.

This was to be the story of Missourians throughout the struggle. Cross the border, accomplish whatever job they thought had to be done, then go back home and brag over jugs of whiskey. These were the men who came to be known as Border Ruffians, Kickapoo Rangers and bushwhackers.

Emigrant aid societies sprang up on both sides of the Mason-Dixon Line. The most famous (and the only one of real consequence) was the New England Emigrant Aid Society. Originally it had been called the Massachusetts Emigrant Aid Society. Masquerading as a force for morality and good, working in the cause of the "Higher Law," it was in reality little more than a money-making scheme—big money and fast money. Eli Thayer, a Massachusetts legislator and successful entrepreneur, was the society's founder. Thayer received a charter from Massachusetts in April 1854 to raise capital in the amount of $5 million. In language of soaring nobility he proposed to fill Kansas "with men who hated slavery and who would drive the hideous thing from the broad and beautiful plains where they were going to raise free homes." He would send twenty thousand settlers per year. Kansas would be saved for God and the North. He spun wonderful visions, dreams of utopia.

And buried within all the fine rhetoric of the society's report were the sentences that got down to basics. Shareholders would have made "an investment which promises large returns at no distant day," and when the company was finally dissolved the transaction would "return a very handsome profit to stockholders upon their investment."

The scheme was to establish boardinghouses and hotels, gristmills and sawmills and commercial centers in general which would become indispensable to the territory and, finally, would be sold for this "very handsome profit" when Kansas achieved statehood. Thayer claimed the venture was likely to pay a profit of 100 percent or more.

The society's motives and methods soon became suspect. Its potential sponsors—that large number of people truly opposed to slavery on moral grounds—were mistrustful. One minister asked if the company was truly benevolent or "a commercial property, a holding and money-making company? . . . Is this matter of shares to be owned by the ministers a mere ruse to get more money? There is an apparent mixture of benevolence, patriotism, and speculation that makes me a little suspicious."

Clerics were not the only doubters, and the society began to flounder. It was saved by Amos Lawrence, a Boston businessman and philanthropist, who became its treasurer and bolstered it with funds from his own pocket and the integrity of his name. It was rechristened the New England Emigrant Aid Society and was off and running again.

The aid society sent out its first party—twenty-nine strong—in July 1854. It elected a site a little below the Kansas River, some forty miles west of Kansas City, Missouri. The next party, numbering sixty-seven and led by Dr. Charles Robinson and Samuel C. Pomeroy, both of whom would play a prominent part in the conflict, arrived at the first settlement in September. From 1854 to 1861 the name of nearly every Free Soil and Pro-slavery man of any stature or wealth was prefixed with a military title. That few had ever served in a legitimate army was considered irrelevant. Shalor Eldridge, a free soil man who arrived in Kansas in February 1855, wrote:

> On approaching Kansas City, Pomeroy, who had had experience in the southwest and appreciated the estimation in which a military title is held in the "land of chivalry," turning to me, said: "Eldridge, if you will address me as 'General' I will reciprocate by calling you 'Colonel.' "It's a bargain," said I.

So much for Officer's Candidate School, Kansas style.

The aid society had named its first settlement Lawrence. It was far from a boom town. In fact, most of a third party that arrived in October 1854 took one look and immediately turned around and went home. Back East they were outspoken in their denunciations of the Honorable Mr. Thayer and his agents. Eldridge described Lawrence this way:

> [We] found the town, so widely known throughout the country, a mere collection of shanties, constructed of sods, grass and clapboards . . . interspersed were some half dozen more substantial rough log cabins. On the bank of the river . . . stood a two-story weather-beaten, second-hand sawmill . . .
>
> In line with the mill, with their rear ends toward the river, stood three structures—buildings they could not be called —of nondescript architecture, each about twenty by fifty or sixty feet in dimensions. Two of them were tents with framework of rough poles thatched with long prairie grass. The middle one . . . was of more elaborate construction, a composite of sod wall and hay tent. The ridgepole of the hay-made roof was supported by a row of rough posts planted in the ground and rising through a platform of unplaned boards. . . . These were the quarters provided by the Emigrant Aid Company for the accommodation of immigrants.

Welcome to Eli Thayer's Utopia.

Governor Andrew H. Reeder arrived in October. He was a ruddy, heavyset man of middle age, a Pennsylvania lawyer, a Democrat down the line. On an abstract level Reeder favored slavery, and he stood 100 percent behind the principle of popular sovereignty. Unfortunately, he was politically and administratively inexperienced. To compound this lack, he naïvely believed that politics on the frontier could not be much different from politics in the East.

Reeder had taken his oath of office in Washington on July 7, 1854, but three months passed before he managed to get himself and a coterie of Pennsylvania associates to the Kansas Territory. Welcomed at Leavenworth with much rhetoric, he responded in kind, took a hasty look at the town, then decided to set up his executive offices at Fort Leavenworth, which was a few miles up river and had been established since 1827.

The Proslavery element expected him to be more or less of a puppet and looked forward to his calling general elections immediately upon his arrival. Geography dictated that a majority of the early settlers would be southern partisans and the Proslavery men wanted to get the voting done before Eli Thayer's promised "20,000 a year" began arriving. Reeder, however, decided to tour the territory first. He dallied away a month, then returned to Leavenworth and called an election for November 29 to select a territorial delegate to Congress. The Proslavery faction was disgruntled—election of a territorial legislature was what they wanted.

There was not much interest in this first election. Washington representation was rather superfluous: *local* government was the big issue. But, as a foreshadowing of things to come, two events of note took place on November 29. First, many Missourians crossed the border to vote (this was strictly illegal, of course), and second, the winner was General J. W. Whitfield, who at the time of his election was a resident of Jackson County, Missouri!

Winter passed without significant incident. Settlers moved in slowly and most people, Free Soil and Pro-slave, spent their time securing their new homes and towns. The Proslavery party pressured Reeder with brazen roughness to call elections. The Free Soilers had their first (eventually of many) disputes. A Territorial Indignation Meeting in January 1855 accused Charles Robinson of going about with armed bands and cutting timber on the claims of other Free Soil men not associated with the society. The meeting charged that "the Emigrant Aid Company of Boston is a swindle on the public, the principal object of those concerned being that of making a grand land speculation under the guise of making Kansas a free state."

Six newspapers were established in the territory—three on each side. The Proslavery view was put forth in the *Leavenworth Herald,* the *Squatter Sovereign* and the *Kansas Pioneer.* Free Soilers had the *Herald of Freedom* (backed by the aid society), the *Kansas Tribune* and the *Kansas Free State.* Large numbers of Missourians were enrolling in the Blue Lodge. Sometimes called The Social Band, Friends' Society, Sons of the South and the Self-Defensives, the Blue Lodge was dedicated to the establishment of slavery in Kansas. The passwords were "Sound on the Goose." The phrase came quickly into public usage and men were judged by whether or not they were SGQ, sound on the goose question: that is, in favor of slavery.

Reeder finally set the election date, March 30, 1855.

Federal census takers arrived because the election of a legislature, unlike that of a territorial delegate, required a precise census. The results of this January–February head-counting revealed that 8,601 settlers were living in Kansas Territory—2,905 of them legal voters.

The election's coming! March 30 will decide whether Kansas Territory goes Free Soil or Slave! A speech Senator Atchison had given in Platte County a few months earlier was still ringing in Missourians' ears:

> All the Territories of the United States [are] to be abolitionized. Colonies are to be planted in all places where slavery and slave institutions can be best assailed; and Kansas is now a favorite position, from whence they can now assail Missouri, Arkansas and Texas. Men are being sent from Massachusetts . . . to seduce, steal and protect fugitive slaves . . .
>
> Should each county in the State of Missouri only do its duty, the question will be decided quietly and peaceably at the ballot box. . . . You cannot watch your stables to prevent thieves from stealing your horses and mules; neither can you watch your negro quarters to prevent your neighbors from seducing away and stealing your negroes.

The good senator concluded by saying he was "opposed to violence—indiscriminate violence," but that he was quite happy to "let the punishment fall on the guilty."

Militant Proslavery man Dr. John Stringfellow—editor of the *Squatter Sovereign*—went back to Missouri to help keep things moving. In a speech at St. Joseph, he told his listeners:

I tell you to mark every scoundrel among you that is the least tainted with freesoilism, or abolitionism, and exterminate him . . . I advise you one and all to enter every election district in Kansas, in defiance of Reeder and his vile myrmidons, and vote at the point of Bowie knife or revolver!

When he gave a similar speech in Boonville, a planter came forward and handed him one thousand dollars saying, "I just sold a nigger for that, and I reckon that's about my share for cleaning out them damned Yankees."

The invasion spirit ran high. The Blue Lodge promised "Free ferry, a dollar a day, and liquor" to all Missourians who would cross into Kansas Territory and vote. One Missouri newspaper editor, Jeb Patterson, found all this a bit too much to stomach. He protested . . . and an enraged mob wrecked his offices and machinery and dumped his type cases into the Missouri River. They threw a rope over a tree and might well have hung him had not his wife interceded.

Missourians were in a voting mood. They began their mass migration two days before the election, large bands of them rolling across the border like herds of buffalo. They came on horseback and by the wagonsful. They came with shotguns, rifles, pistols, Bowie knives and large supplies of whiskey, and they came with two cannons loaded with musket balls. The ferries could not handle their numbers and the riverboat *New Lucy* was pressed into service.

The *Kansas Free State* wrote, " . . . the population of Lawrence [500] was increased to near 1,500 in two days.

The roads were cut up very much with wagons, and the atmosphere was filled with smoke from their campfires." In an admirable attempt to be fair, the *Kansas Free State* went on to say that considering the great numbers of arms among them and the amount of alcohol, the Missourians were well behaved. Free Soilers assumed this was due to the authority of their leaders and the precision of their organization.

This observation was correct. The campaign was excellently planned. The voting army was divided into several units, each of which went to a specific election district in numbers large enough to insure that the Free Soil vote would be overwhelmed. Although the threat of mayhem was omnipresent, the relative lack of actual violence that day is remarkable.

The election itself was a fiasco. In some cases, district judges merely swallowed whatever scruples they might have had and received the vote of everyone who stepped forward and claimed to be qualified. Others were more conscionable, but their resistance was an irritant rather than an obstacle to the Missourians. In Bloomington the judges did not take the hint that their resignations were in order. So, while his companions drew knives and revolvers, a Border Ruffian took out his watch and gave the judges five minutes—after which they could resign or die. The judges resigned and were promptly replaced with Proslavery men. Such activity was the order of the day.

When the results were in—well, hallelujah, boys! Thirty-six Proslavery legislators (the majority of whom lived in Missouri) had been elected, and three Free Soilers had somehow managed to squeak in.

The results also revealed (and the Proslavery party didn't consider this an embarrassment at all) that *6,307 votes had been cast.* Investigation at a much later date further disclosed that of the territory's 2,905 legal voters only 1,410 had voted, which left a total of 4,997 illegal votes!

The Proslavery party liked the number. They thought it showed a very clear-cut majority.

"ALL HAIL! Proslavery Party Victorious!" cried the *Leavenworth Herald.* "Come on, Southern men! Bring your slaves and fill up the Territory. Kansas is saved. Abolitionism is rebuked, her fortress stormed, her flag is draggling in the dust!"

Not exactly, but close to it. The *Kansas Free State,* still trying to be honest, admitted that though many Free Soilers had been stopped from voting, there were "from seventy-five to one hundred Eastern emigrants, just arrived, who voted the Free-State ticket. This we tried to prevent, but could not." Those Proslavery men who felt they had to justify their conduct (very few) bandied this fact about loudly. They also pointed out that of the eighteen election districts only six protested to Governor Reeder. But they neglected to mention that William Philips, a Leavenworth Free Soil lawyer who instigated one of the protests, was kidnapped and taken across the river to Weston, Missouri, where he was tarred and feathered and then ridden on a rail with his head shaved to an auction block where he was sold by a drunken clowning slave for one dollar. This and other reasons that could be enumerated by the clicks of cocking revolvers accounted for the fact that only six districts protested.

Although Governor Reeder's ethics were questionable in areas of personal finance—which caused his eventual recall—he was high-principled in politics. And he was appalled. The governor testified that he had been threatened with death if he should interfere. Charles Robinson wrote to Amos Lawrence four days after the election: "The election is awful, and will no doubt be set aside. So says the governor, although his life is threatened if he doesn't comply with the Missourians' demands. I with others shall act as his body-guard."

The day Reeder canvassed the returns, the thirty-six Proslavery legislators lined one side of the executive chambers, heavily armed. Reeder and fourteen friends sat on the other side, also armed. A brace of cocked pistols lay on the table next to the governor's papers.

Reeder set aside the results from each of the protesting districts, voiding them on grounds of "technical irregularities." He ordered new elections held on May 22, then left the territory on April 17, ostensibly to attend to personal matters in Pennsylvania and to consult with the President in Washington.

Missourians were not much interested in the May 22 elections. They had contingency plans for any Free Soilers elected and thus, with the voting relatively honest, eight Free Soilers were put into office.

The South was roaring support for Missouri and the territory's Proslavery party. The *Mobile Register* wrote, "We trust that the Missourians will continue the good fight they have begun, and, if need be, call on their brethren in the South for help to put down by force of arms the infernal schemes hatched in Northern hot-beds of abolition for their injury." The *Charleston Mercury* warned that "Hireling emigrants are poured in to extinguish this new hope of the South." The Democratic State convention of Georgia expressed its "sympathy with the friends of slavery in Kansas in their manly efforts to maintain the rights and interests of the Southern people over the paid adventurers and Jesuitical hordes of Northern abolitionism."

In Washington, President Pierce suggested Reeder resign. Reeder said no.

During spring and summer, numerous heavy boxes marked "books" were unloaded from side-wheelers in Kansas City and shipped by freight wagons to various citizens of Lawrence, Kansas Territory. These boxes contained Sharps rifles—extremely efficient breech-loading weapons, the newest and best firearm available. In early June, Free Soilers gathered and drafted a memorial to Congress protesting that "men armed with guns, revolvers and bowie knives, from another state," had controlled the elections of March 30. They also passed a resolution: "In reply to the threats of war so frequently made in our neighboring State, our answer is, 'We Are Ready!'" And military companies began drilling in Lawrence.

Reeder returned to Kansas in late June, in time to attend the opening of the territorial legislature at Pawnee. The site was Reeder's. It lay more than 125 miles west of the Missouri border, in the middle of nowhere. The governor had designated it the capital of Kansas Territory.

And he had a sound reason. He had bought most of the land there and also owned part of the Pawnee Town

Company, which had erected a two-storey Capitol Building and two claptrap boarding sheds. In time he would make an impressive sum of money. But now, except for Fort Riley two miles away, there was nothing around but empty, rolling plains. The legislators muttered and glowered at Reeder but there was work to do, so they set up tents and sleeping bags, cooked over open fires, opened their session and came right to the major order of business.

As of May 22, there had been twenty-eight Proslavery legislators and eleven Free Soil. Freesoiler Martin Conway had resigned before the Pawnee meeting. He wrote:

> Instead of recognizing this as the legislature of Kansas and participating in its proceedings as such, I utterly repudiate it, and repudiate it as derogatory to the respectablity of popular government . . . I am ready to set its assumed authority at defiance, and shall be prompt to spurn and trample under my feet its insolent enactments whenever they conflict with my rights or inclinations.

That was fine with the Proslavery men: one down, ten to go.

They declared that Reeder had had no right to disregard the election of March 30. Therefore, they reasoned, the elections of May 22 were null and void. That enabled them to unseat the eight Free Soil winners of May and to replace them with the original Proslavery men.

Nine down, two to go.

They ousted another Free Soiler on a technicality. One to go.

But this last man was stubborn. He hung on for another month. Then he resigned, stating that "to retain a seat in such circumstances would be . . . a condescension too inglorious for the spirit of an American freeman."

Kansas Territory Legislature: Sound on the Goose to a man.

The only other business conducted was to pass a resolution changing the territorial Capital to Shawnee Mission, which was just across the border from Westport, Missouri—within walking distance, some cynics noted, of many of the legislators' Missouri homes.

Governor Reeder immediately vetoed the bill.

The legislature immediately passed it over his veto.

Shawnee Mission was the capital of Kansas Territory.

The lawmakers grew homesick after only four days— a malady that became even more poignant when they heard reports of a cholera outbreak in the Pawnee area. They adjourned, to reconvene at Shawnee Mission on July 16.

Governor Reeder openly broke with the legislature. When "they removed from Reeder's town to somebody else's town," as Senator Toombs of Georgia said, they evidently committed the most heinous and unforgivable of offenses.

Reeder was officially removed from office by a letter from Washington dated July 28, 1855. Referral was made to his land speculations (he was involved in several) and "Pawnee City" was cited in specific. Reeder was never prosecuted, but his partner, Major W. R. Montgomery, the commandant of Fort Riley, was court-martialed and dismissed from the service.

The legislature made one noteworthy accomplishment that summer at Shawnee Mission: they enacted a code of laws. Laboring mightily, they copied the Missouri code word for word, striking out "State of Missouri" whenever it occurred and substituting "Territory of Kansas."

They made one other modification when, to their horror, they discovered that Missouri's laws regarding slavery were far, far too liberal. So they stiffened them up in the Territorial Code. When they were done, a man who kidnapped a free Negro and sold him into slavery could get a tough two years in prison. But a man who helped a slave escape would be executed. And a man could be thrown in jail for reading a newspaper of Free Soil leanings. And a man could have his property confiscated for questioning the right of other men to hold slaves. And a man could lose his vote by refusing to take an oath to uphold the Fugitive Slave Law.

And the governor could pardon no offenses around the issue of slavery. After all, the law was the law. Reeder vetoed the code, but it was passed over his veto.

A southern lawyer wrote in the *Montgomery Register:*

> They now have laws more efficient to protect slave property than any State in the Union. These laws have just taken effect, and have already silenced the Abolitionists; for, in spite of their heretofore boasting, they know they will be enforced to the very letter with utmost vigor.

Vigor, that was the word. And both sides were getting ready to use a lot of it.

3.

THE OPENING SHOTS

The summer of 1855 passed without serious incident. In Atchison, the hotbed of Proslavery sentiment, a giant Border Ruffian named Thomason nearly beat a Free Soiler to death. When a transient minister, Reverend Pardee Butler, refused to sign a memorial commending Thomason's defense of God and Country, Atchison's good citizens hauled the preacher to the river, roughed him up, then lashed him to two cottonwood poles and set him adrift.

Governor Wilson Shannon arrived two weeks later to pick up where Reeder had abruptly left off. He was warmly welcomed in Atchison. Stringfellow, who in addition to being editor of the *Squatter Sovereign* was also the legislature's Speaker of the House, assured the new governor that: "Here no Catalines abound. There are no lean and hungry Italians with their treacherous smiles, no cowards with their stilettos, no assassins of reputation."

Slaves were animals, mulattoes not much better. Abolitionists were scum, Mormons hardly more desirable. Indians were to be pushed back, and now the new governor could rest easy, he was told, for there were no treacherous stiletto-wielding Italians in the territory. This was truly democratic bigotry.

Stringfellow continued with, "Yes, here, Your Excellency, the morning prayer is heard on every hill, the evening orison is chanted in every valley and glen."

Kansas Territory according to Stringfellow: Paradise Regained.

Governor Shannon tendered his thanks and expressed his conviction that Kansas was indeed a wondrous and peaceful land, and that it was the duty of all citizens to obey the laws enacted by the late and thoroughly legal legislature and that it was his duty to enforce those laws.

Wilson Shannon—Sound on the Goose.

The Proslavery party welcomed him with open arms.

Free Soilers choked.

Shannon was an Ohioan by birth, a lawyer who had married judiciously and had done moderately well in the Democratic party, holding a succession of minor offices, then serving one term as governor of Ohio, later minister to Mexico, then congressman in Washington. His support of the Kansas-Nebraska Bill alienated his liberal constituency and he was not reelected. He returned to the practice of law. When Reeder was removed, the governorship was offered to another Pennsylvanian, who declined the honor. Shannon made application for the post and was appointed.

So on September 3, 1855, Wilson Shannon arrived in Kansas Territory, eager, smiling, employed—a man overly fond of alcohol, a weak man who had been used before as a foil by stronger personalities and would most certainly be used so again.

James H. Lane was one of the dominant figures in the territory's history, and as Machiavellian a character as could be hoped for. He was born in Indiana in 1814, the son of a prominent politician. He practiced law, fought in the Mexican War with the rank of colonel, served as lieutenant-governor of Indiana and then went to Washington as a congressman. His career took a bad turn in early 1855, due in large part to his support of the Kansas–Nebraska Act, and he emigrated to Kansas Territory, arriving a few months before Shannon.

Passing through Westport, Missouri, he told a questioner that he would "as soon buy a nigger as a mule." He meant it. Slavery in Kansas Territory was not a question of ethics to Jim Lane but merely a matter of climate. If the weather was suitable for slaves, then he had no objections to slavery in the territory. He had come to Kansas for one reason—to organize the Democratic party and to obtain a position of importance within it. The paramount concern of James H. Lane was the future of James H. Lane.

But he ran into a brick wall. The party was already well established, thank you, and Atchison, Stringfellow and a few others provided more than enough leadership. Lane made several sallies, but accomplished absolutely nothing. James H. Lane was a man without a party in the early summer of 1855.

He found this unacceptable and immediately set out

to rectify the situation. Results were not long in coming. The *Free State,* describing a Free Soil meeting on July 17, wrote that "among the counselors who were caught on the wing was Colonel Lane, fresh from attendance upon the bogus legislature."

Free Soilers were naturally mistrustful of him. But Lane was subtle, devious and persuasive and possessed a certain charisma—that enigmatic quality that makes men cheer and stamp their feet, that makes men swell the ranks and go marching off to the music of drums and fifes.

A month later we find him addressing another Free Soil meeting in an earnest, sincere and, one suspects, oily tone:

Mr. President:

If I believed a prayer from me would do any good it would be that you might be imbued with the wisdom of Solomon, the caution of Washington, and the justice of Franklin. . . . It requires wisdom, it requires manhood to restrain passion. I say it as a citizen of Kansas, I wish we had wisdom today. . . . I believe it is the duty of each of us to define our position. I am here as anxious as any of you to secure a free constitution for Kansas. A lesson I received from childhood was never to speak of man or woman unless I could speak well of them. It is represented that I came to Kansas to retrieve my political fortunes, but you, gentlemen, should know that I was urgently solicited to be a candidate for another term of Congress, but I positively declined. . . . I desire Kansas to be a free state.

But earnest and sincere speeches were not enough to win over the Free Soilers. This was fine with Lane. He wasn't a man to whom humility came easily. His native style was bombastic. And he cut loose with it shortly after his first address.

Senator John Ingalls later described Lane's speeches this way:

> His voice is a series of transitions from the broken scream of a maniac to the hoarse, rasping gutturals of a Dutch butcher in the last gasp of inebriation; the construction of his sentences is loose and disjointed; his diction is a pudding of slang, profanity and solecism; and yet the electric shock of his extraordinary eloquence thrills like the blast of a trumpet; the magnetism of his manner, the fire of his glance, the studied earnestness of his utterances, find a sudden response in the will of his audience, and he sways them like a field of reeds shaken by the wind.

The man was physically striking. He was well above six feet and had dark, intense eyes. His hair was fine, his forehead high. He had a sharp nose and a square jaw, and his body was angular and lanky. "His energy," according to Ingalls, "was tireless and his activity indefatigable. No night was too dark, no storm too wild, no heat or cold too excessive, no distance too great, to delay his meteoric pilgrimages, with dilapidated garb and equipage, across the trackless prairies from convention to convention."

He captured the Free Soilers. The *Kansas City Times* reported the pivotal speech:

> The crowd was immense. The hour came and the people to hear. Lane was in his best mood. He was prepared for a vituperative, sarcastic, ironical and intensely personal

speech. . . . Such an analysis of character was never heard
before or since in Kansas. . . . His late Democratic associates
were denounced, burlesqued, ridiculed and pilloried in a
hysteria of laughter by an excited, cyclonic crowd. No one
ever afterward doubted where Lane stood. He crossed with
a leap the Rubicon of radical politics and burned all his
bridges behind him. He was not baptized—he was im-
mersed in the foaming floods of radicalism.

Lane, the man who would as soon buy a nigger as a
mule, was for Free Soil. And Free Soil was for Lane.

Charles Robinson was not happy. Up to now, the Emigrant Aid Society agent had been the most influential
man in the Free Soil party. Rarely is a man pushed into
second place so quickly. And Robinson, though far from
a paragon of morality in business, which eventually made
him one of the richest men in the territory and later the
state, was morally horrified by slavery. Lane on the other
hand viewed human bondage as a bright rubber ball to
be juggled whichever way the fans wanted. This made
Robinson's displacement all the more bitter.

The two men would work together and lead others
in a common cause, but they would be rivals, even enemies, all their lives.

Big Springs was a little west of Lawrence, a cross-
roads with four or five clapboard shacks and log cabins.
One hundred Free Soil delegates met there on September 5. Nearly three hundred spectators appeared to watch.
The purpose was to weld all the various antislavery elements into one, cohesive body, the Free State party. This
involved the hammering out of a party platform.

It was here that Lane persuaded the assembly, against the impassioned arguments of Robinson, to include the Black Law in the party platform. This law called for the *permanent exclusion of each and every Negro, slave or free, from the Kansas Territory.*

The delegates were pleased on two counts: first, they thought it would refute the South's charge that Free Soilers were "nigger-stealing abolitionists," and second, they would never have to compete against slave labor. The resolution was passed by a vote of 99 to 1.

A strongly worded platform was drafted, its resolutions written by ex-Governor Reeder, who had returned to run as the Free State candidate for territorial delegate to Congress.

A few days earlier the legislature, just before adjourning, had stated the following: "*Be it resolved* by the House of Representatives, the Council concurring therein, That it is the duty of the Pro-Slavery party, the Union-loving men of Kansas Territory, to know but one issue, Slavery; and that any party making or attempting to make any other, is, and should be held, as an ally of Abolitionism and disunionism."

The Free State party happily accepted slavery as the issue, even though most of the Free Soilers were not abolitionists. At Big Springs Reeder pulled out all the stops. He termed the legislature a "monstrous consummation of an act of violence, usurpation, and fraud . . . a contemptible and hypocritical mockery of republicanism. . . . We owe no allegiance or obedience to the tyrannical enactments of this spurious legislature."

Many of his contemporaries later gave him the dubious honor of having signaled the start of open warfare when he penned a resolution that read: "Whenever peaceful remedies shall fail and forcible measures shall furnish any reasonable prospect of success, then let our now shrinking and reluctant hostility be pushed to a bloody issue!"

The legislature set October 1 as the election date for a territorial delegate. The Free State party called an election on October 9. Reeder received more votes than his opponent, J. W. Whitfield, but the Free State election was called illegal, and Governor Shannon certified Whitfield in the post. Reeder protested to Congress, which investigated and decided against him. Reeder and other Free Soilers were subsequently indicted for treason by the grand jury of Douglas County (in which Lawrence was located) and had to flee the territory.

The Free State party assembled at the new town of Topeka on October 23 to hold a constitutional convention, and elected Jim Lane as convention president. They drafted a constitution which contained a clause that would prohibit slavery from the territory after July 4, 1857. Lane fought against a proposal that certain "approved" Indians be granted suffrage, but he was defeated and the right to vote was given by the Topeka constitution to "every civilized male Indian who has adopted the habits of the white man." He succeeded, however, in having the Black Law written into the document. This provided for closing Kansas to all Negroes, slave or free, as soon as the territory became a state.

William Phillips, a reporter for the *New York Tribune,* described one of the most active Black Law men at the convention. He was the Reverend J. M. Tuttle, who was never seen without his rifle. Phillips wrote: "He was . . . opposed to allowing slave owners more than a year to take their slaves from the territory, declaring, 'I kem to Kansas to live in a free state and I don't want niggers a-trampin' over my grave!' "

The Topeka Convention adjourned after selecting December 15 as the day the constitution would be submitted to the people and March 4, 1856, as the day an opposition Free Soil government was to be organized.

Proslavery forces promptly met at Leavenworth, denounced the Topeka meeting as treasonable, and with Governor William Shannon presiding, formed themselves into the Law and Order party to combat the Free State party.

Although there had been several incidents of outrage and violence on both sides, only three deaths attributable to the slave issue had occurred. Free Soiler Lucius Kibbee killed Missourian Henry Davis, who had burned a Free Soiler's home and threatened Kibbee with a knife. Free Soiler Cole McCrea killed Proslavery Malcolm Clark following an argument in which Clark had clubbed McCrea with a two-by-four. And Proslavery Pat Laughlin killed Free Soiler Collins in a brawl.

But the killing that turned both sides into armies was the fourth one, which occurred on November 21, 1855.

Free Soiler Charles Dow and Proslavery Franklin Coleman came up against each other with brandished weapons over a disputed tract of hardwood at Hickory Point, a dozen miles south of Lawrence. But both men eased off and nothing came of it. A few days later, though, Coleman encountered Dow and blasted a load of shotgun slugs into him.

Free Soilers were furious, particularly since Sheriff Samuel Jones of Douglas County, a Proslavery man who lived in Westport, Missouri, and was the postmaster there, made no move to arrest Coleman. Free Soilers began to talk of lynching. Coleman lived in Palmyra, a small town on the tip of Hickory Point. Twenty other Proslavery families lived there too, outnumbered by the Free Soil men in town and thoroughly darkened by the long shadow of Lawrence.

Coleman fled to Shawnee Mission and surrendered himself to Governor Shannon. He'd killed Dow in self-defense, he claimed, and two of his neighbors, Buckley and Hargis, would testify that Dow had attacked him with a wagon skein.

Old Jacob Branson, with whom Dow had boarded, captained a band of Kansas Regulators, a kind of Free Soil militia. Branson and seventy-five men rode to Hargis's home, where Buckley and other Proslavery men had gathered. They called out Hargis and Buckley and demanded to know what testimony they would give.

Self-defense.

Dow, it was pointed out, had been some fifty yards away when Coleman shot him down. Hargis and Buckley were either lying or had very strange ideas about self-defense. The Free Soil men gave them until Sunday night to change their minds. Hargis and Buckley wisely elected to leave the area. They took their families back to Missouri, then went to Shawnee Mission where they related the threat to Sheriff Jones and Governor Shannon.

When the Free Soilers returned for Hargis and Buckley's answer, they were angered to discover the men had fled. A proposition to fire their homes was voted down, but the cabins burned that night anyway.

A man rode to Shawnee to warn Buckley and Hargis not to return, that the Free Soilers would kill them.

Sheriff Jones was delighted with this turn of events. He called out a well-armed posse of nine Westport Missourians, obtained a peace warrant against Branson and rode out to arrest him.

The posse dragged Branson from his bed at 2 A.M., sat him on a saddleless mule and headed toward Lecompton, the county seat of Douglas County as well as the new territorial capital. Five miles from Lawrence, at Blanton's Bridge across the Wakarusa, a party of Free Soil men stopped the posse. Hargis and Buckley in later affidavits estimated the number of rescuers between thirty and forty. Jones's deposition said "some 40." They were armed, according to the reports of the Sheriff and his men, with: Sharps rifles, double-barreled shotguns, pistols, Bowie knives and swords—barely able to walk, so weighted down with weaponry.

Actually, there were only fifteen men in the rescue party, and while most were armed, there were not enough weapons for everyone and some carried clubs and stones.

But fifteen or forty, bristling with arms or not, the result was the same—Branson was spirited away.

Sheriff Jones was both angry and jubilant. He had lost his prisoner, but had gained a fine excuse to wipe Lawrence off the map—something he had long and intensely desired to do. So this eager young man, who was on record as wanting to "corral all the abolitionists

and make pets of them," rode to Franklin with his posse
and from there sent couriers to Atchison, Leavenworth
and Kickapoo as well as numerous towns in Missouri.
Men and guns he wanted, and as many as he could get.

Someone pointed out that it might seem odd to sum-
mon aid from a neighboring state without even so much
as notifying the governor of the Kansas Territory. Re-
luctantly, Jones had to concede the point.

He dashed off a short dispatch to Governor Shannon,
which he ended by saying; "You may consider an open
rebellion as having already commenced, and I call upon
you for three thousand men to carry out the laws."

Jones was going to give Free Soilers their death blow.
Proslavery men smelled blood in the air and they
mounted up and rode off by the hundreds to crush the
life from Abolitionism.

4.

THE WAKARUSA WAR

Hastily printed flyers were tacked to trees, farmhouses, general stores and saloons all along the Missouri border. They read:

TO ARMS! TO ARMS!

It is expected that every lover of Law and Order will rally at Leavenworth, on Saturday, December 1, 1855, prepared to march at once to the scene of the rebellion, to put down the outlaws of Douglas county, who are committing depredation upon persons and property, burning down houses and declaring open hostility to the laws, and have forcibly rescued a prisoner from the Sheriff. Come one, come all! The outlaws, it is said, are armed to the teeth, and number 1,000 men. Every man should bring his rifle and ammunition, and it would be well to bring two or three days' provision. Every man to his post, and to his duty.

MANY CITIZENS

The Blue Lodges went into action. The Liberty, Missouri, chapter alone enrolled two hundred men and subscribed over a thousand dollars. The message was quite clear and Missourians were not slow in responding.

Jones's request to Shannon for aid was dated November 27. On that same day, shortly after he received the message, Shannon contacted the commanding officers of the Kansas militia, told them that Free Soilers were in open rebellion and requested them to report with their forces to Sheriff Jones without delay.

In later years, Shannon spent a good deal of time trying to explain his actions while governor. Most of his behavior and decisions, particularly during the Wakarusa War, were either bumbling, panicky or downright stupid. He firmly believed, he subsequently stated, that Branson's rescue was the signal for a well-planned revolution. To be fair, he probably *did* believe a civil war was in the offing—Wilson Shannon believed practically anything.

Shannon claimed he never expected Missourians to cross the border and march on Lawrence. However, the Kansas territorial militia at full strength could muster little more than fifty men and it is curious to wonder just where Shannon thought Jones's "3,000" were going to come from.

On December 1, Leavenworth was an armed camp. Missourians swarmed through the town, were bivouacked in semiorganized military companies on its outskirts, were pouring across the border hourly. On that same day, Governor Shannon telegraphed President Pierce asking authority to call out the First Cavalry, which was stationed at Fort Leavenworth.

He then sent a message to Colonel E. V. Sumner, commanding officer of the First Cavalry, and asked him to ready himself for a march to Lawrence. Sumner replied that he would be ready to move just as soon as he received authorization from Washington.

On December 2, Shannon wrote to Sheriff Jones and ordered him to wait for the federal troops. It is evident that Shannon's prime wish *was* to protect the peace, for in this and in other communications, he ordered, cautioned and implored the Proslavery leaders to use restraint and he insisted that law and order and protection of the peace was their goal.

But Shannon's goal was not the goal of the Border Army, fifteen hundred men strong, camped outside Lawrence on December 3. A Missouri captain told the *Tribune's* Phillips, "We mean to have Kansas. And we are going to have it, if we have to wade through blood to our knees to get it." Shannon wrote the President, after he had visited one of the Missourian's camps: *I found a deep and settled feeling of hostility against the opposing forces in Lawrence and apparently a fixed determination to attack the place and demolish it.* And after the affair was over Sheriff Jones said, "If Shannon had not been such a damned fool, we would have wiped out Lawrence."

Charles Robinson had recognized the seriousness of the situation from the first. He called an emergency meeting the morning after Jacob Branson's rescue. A committee of safety was appointed with Robinson at its head. Policy, outlined by the conservative Robinson, was agreed upon. The citizens of Lawrence would disavow all responsibility for the rescue. Those residents who had been involved were speedily sent out of town, so Jones and the Missourians would have no pretext for an invasion. The Free Soilers would adopt a strictly defensive posture, would offer no provocation to the Border Army.

Military arrangements were made. Since most Lawrencians were thinking upon lines similar to Robinson's, he was given the rank of major general and made commander-in-chief of the Free Soil force. Lane, with his past military experience, was obviously the best qualified to command, but his volatile character and impulsive temper made him too great a risk. He was appointed brigadier general, second in command. The half-finished Free State Hotel was designated command post.

Lawrence's fighting force was only two hundred fifty strong. When the Border Army's size was learned, Free Soilers sent appeals for help to other towns. Larger settlements responded with whole companies and individual Free Soilers or small parties of them arrived daily. At its peak, the Free Soil army in Lawrence numbered six hundred.

The Border Ruffians gathered into two camps, the main body on the Wakarusa near Franklin, three miles southeast of Lawrence, and the other at Lecompton, ten miles to the northwest. On Sunday, Jones received Shannon's order to wait for federal help. The Sheriff did wait, but not because of Shannon—he was no longer sure his army could take Lawrence.

Lawrence was now buttressed by four large earth and wood forts connected to each other by rifle pits. The number of Free Soil defenders was variously reported to be from five hundred to fifteen hundred. Jones was inclined to believe the latter figure. And it was definitely known that there were two hundred Sharps rifles in the town—

weapons that woefully outclassed anything the Missourians had. In addition, the Free Soldiers had managed to smuggle in a brass howitzer, which, the encamped army well knew, was not to be trifled with.

It appeared for the moment to be a deadlock.

Supplies were eaten away and inactivity began to weigh heavily on the Missourians. They turned to the countryside and laid it to waste. They robbed travelers, plundered cabins, fired haystacks and stole all the horses and cattle they could find.

There was unrest within Lawrence too. The town could not support its swollen population. Nerves were strained. A young woman wrote:

> It looked strange . . . to see the streets paraded from morning till night by men in military array; to see them toil day and night throwing up intrenchments; to see them come in to their meals each with his gun in hand and sometimes bringing it to the tables. . . . How we toiled to feed the multitudes, seldom snatching a moment to look out upon the strange scenes—often asking, "What are the prospects today?"—or at midnight as, worn and weary, we sought the pillow, discussing such themes as these . . . "There's prospect of an attack to-night." "The guard has been doubled . . ."

Missourians, no longer amused by pillaging, began agitating for an attack. Shannon's nerves were in bad shape. Then on December 4, he heard from President Franklin Pierce: he could have the federal troops just as soon as the Secretary of War could make out the orders. Greatly relieved, Shannon notified Colonel Sumner at

Fort Leavenworth. Early the next morning, Sumner replied that he would march with his regiment in a few hours.

Shannon was in good cheer, confident that the mess would soon be over, neatly tied with federal ribbon. He was stunned by a message from Sheriff Jones who wrote that he had learned the Lawrence defenders were not half as strong as reported and that he intended to enter the town tomorrow.

Today, Wednesday, December 5, Shannon realized with horror, was Jones's "tomorrow."

To the governor's further despair two Free Soilers arrived at his quarters. They did a fine job of pleading their case, convincing him that it was a foreign army threatening Lawrence, that neither Branson nor any of his rescuers were in town, that the Lawrencians had made no aggressive move, had not fired a single shot despite the fact that their pickets had been fired upon repeatedly, wanted only to live in peace.

Shannon was shocked by the fact that the bulk of Jones's army had come from Missouri and had come with the avowed intention to destroy Lawrence. He assured the emissaries that all he desired was a peaceful solution and that he would arrive shortly with federal troops to guarantee that one was reached. The Free Soilers rode back to Lawrence with the good news.

Shannon, confident that Sumner's dragoons would soon be on the march, went to Westport and persuaded some influential Missourians to accompany him and help keep their fellow citizens in check. He suffered a near crushing blow to his morale when a rider from Fort Leavenworth overtook the party and handed him a note from Sumner.

"On more mature reflection," Sumner wrote, "I think it will not be proper for me to move until I receive the orders of the government."

A despondent William Shannon reached the heart of the Proslavery Wakarusa camp at three o'clock on Thursday morning. There he received the only welcome news in an otherwise dismal day: Lawrence, contrary to his fears, had not yet been attacked.

It did not take him long to feel the warlike pulse of the Missourians. He sent a desperate note to Colonel Sumner imploring him to come even if he had not yet received orders from Washington.

But Sumner was not going to stick his neck out. He began his reply: "I regret extremely to disappoint you . . . " No orders, no troops.

The Border Army distrusted Shannon, and they did not want federal troops. Soldiers would, of course, prevent them from taking Lawrence. Also, many Missourians were carrying arms recently stolen from a government arsenal. They had no desire to be found with such weapons.

Shannon met with Jones and other Border Army leaders. The governor seemed to be the only person present who wished to resolve the conflict without a gush of blood. Ex-Senator David R. Atchison, who had lost his bid for re-election earlier in the year and who was now commanding a company of riflemen at the Wakarusa camp, finally brought the Missourians more or less under control. Having had a little time to think, Atchison realized that an attack on Lawrence might well be disastrous for Proslavery forces throughout the country.

He took the governor's side and argued: "If you attack Lawrence now, you attack it as a mob. And what would

be the result? You would cause the election of an abolitionist president and the ruin of the Democratic Party.
Wait a little. You cannot now destroy these people without losing more than you can gain."

The Border Army didn't like it. They had come to fight.
But Atchison's influence was large and his loyalties beyond
question. Also, the significance of his words was clear. He
had told them to wait a little—even the slowest Missourian could draw the proper conclusion: *perhaps later
you can destroy these people without losing anything.*

Shannon had time to breathe, but the crisis was still far
from over.

On Friday, December 7, Wilson Shannon went to
Lawrence. A few high-ranking members of the Border
Army—including Colonel Albert Boone, grandson of the
famous Daniel Boone—went with him.

The Free Soilers were in a foul mood. One of them,
Thomas Barber, had been killed by members of the Border
Army the night before. Barber and two friends had gone
to visit their families, seven miles outside of Lawrence.
They blundered into a dozen Proslavery men. The Free
Soilers claimed Barber had been shot without provocation,
murdered. The Proslavery men said he'd been killed in a
fair fight. Lawrencians found it difficult to believe that
three Free Soilers would, or could, engage twelve Missourians in a fair fight.

Governor Shannon was not optimistic, particularly
since the meeting place was the Free State Hotel—in
which the body of Thomas Barber was laid out for all to
see. Nothing was accomplished. The minimum demand
of the Proslavery party was the surrender of the Sharps

rifles. The Free Soilers refused to give up what they called private property, which they well knew to be their major source of strength against their antagonists.

Shannon returned to the Wakarusa camp dejected. On Saturday morning leaders of the Border Army informed the governor that unless the Free Soilers surrendered their arms, Lawrence would be attacked that very day. Desperate, Shannon got the Proslavery men to appoint a committee of thirteen men who could act for the Border Army. They were to wait at Franklin. Shannon would bring Free Soil representatives there to hammer out a compromise.

The governor then returned to the Free State Hotel. After several hours, he and Free Soil leaders drafted a document, which was signed by Shannon, Robinson and Lane. It was a vaguely worded thing that spoke of a "misunderstanding," stated that Lawrencians had not organized to resist the law, pledged to support "proper authority" and "legal process" and ended with the statement: "We wish it understood, that we do not herein express any opinion as to the validity of the enactments of the Territorial Legislature."

When this was read to the men defending Lawrence, an intense, grim-faced man known as Old Brown (of whom more will be said later) leaped upon a box, shouted "Those laws we denounce and spit upon and will never obey!" and began a passionate, bloody harangue against the Proslavery forces. He was pulled down by Lane's and Robinson's men. The two Free Soil generals explained that by "proper authority" and "legal process" they were referring to the federal government. Most Free Soilers were satisfied. Old Brown and his sons were not—they left Lawrence in disgust.

The Proslavery delegates in Franklin were not pleased. But Shannon insisted that, as the document in hand claimed, Branson's rescue had not been made with the knowledge and consent of the Lawrence citizenry and that Lawrencians would not resist the law. The Sharps rifles, the governor said, *were* private property and the Free Soilers were justified in their refusal to surrender them.

Shannon ordered the Border Army to disband. The volunteers were outraged. "Shannon has played us false!" Stringfellow shouted. "The Yankees have tricked us. The Governor of Kansas has disgraced himself and the whole pro-slavery party." Ex-Senator Atchison told his fellow Missourians, "Boys, we cannot fight now. The position the Lawrence people have taken is such that it would not do to make an attack upon it. . . . But boys, we will fight some time, by God!"

The Border Army might still have launched an attack that night, but the weather turned suddenly bitter. The wind drove cutting rain and sleet down against the encamped Missourians. The men huddled about their fires. In the morning, feeling betrayed, and suffering in the freezing elements, the Border Army broke up, and men wrapped in great coats and blankets began making their way back home to their wives and fires and warm beds.

On Sunday, December 9, Governor Wilson Shannon returned to Lawrence once again, this time as the guest of honor at a gala party. The governor imbibed quite freely and was in a jolly mood. When the merriment was

at its height, about ten o'clock in the evening, Charles
Robinson, who had gone out to get a breath of fresh air,
came dashing back in with the shocking news that a mob
of Border Ruffians was drawing in for an attack on Lawrence.

Shannon was the epitome of outrage and indignation.
Robinson claimed the governor's protection and requested
permission to repel the invasion. Shannon consented instantly. Robinson requested such authority in writing so
"that it might not appear hereafter, if a recounter should
take place, as if we were acting against, rather than with
the approbation of the territorial executive."

A paper was produced. Someone rushed up with a pen.
Shannon did not bother to read the statement, but signed
it with a flourish.

What he signed was this:

To C. H. Robinson and James H. Lane, Commanders of the
enrolled Citizens of Lawrence: You are hereby authorized
and directed to take such measures and use the enrolled
forces under your command in such a manner, for the
preservation of the peace and the protection of the persons
and property of Lawrence and its vicinity, as, in your judge-
ment, shall best secure that end.

The governor was the only person in town surprised
to find that the night, when he rushed into the street, was
as quiet and peaceful as any man could have wished for.

The governor left Lawrence humiliated and dispirited:
it seemed that all that was required to make a fool of him
these days was the desire to do so.

5.

THE FREE SOIL CAUSE IS CLUBBED

On December 15, 1855, Free Soilers flocked to the polls and voted nearly to a man to ratify the constitution that had been drafted in October at Topeka. Proslavery men left them alone and watched with mild amusement, as if the Free Soilers were playing some childish game. The only violence occurred at Leavenworth, where Free Soilers were a marked minority. A gang of Proslavery men demanded the ballot box. When the election judges refused, the southern sympathizers kicked down the door, crashed through the windows, beat up the Free Soilers and absconded with the ballot box.

Christmas morning found Kansas Territory blanketed wth snow, the air crisp and stinging. The day of the Lord's birth was celebrated by an editorial in the *Kansas Pioneer*. "Season's Greetings," it said, then proceeded to scourge abolitionists and called upon all law-abiding men who loved their country to come to Kansas and kill every Free Soiler just as soon as that God-forsaken person set foot in Kansas.

Election of Free Soil officers was scheduled for January 15. In Easton, the election was delayed until the seventeenth because of rumors that a company of Kickapoo Rangers was going to stage a raid. A few armed Free State men led by Captain R. P. Brown (no relation to Old Brown) rode to Easton to protect their friends. Taunts were exchanged, then threats, then gunfire, and when it was over a Proslavery man lay dead.

Kickapoo Rangers took to their saddles and raced for Easton. They captured Captain Brown the next morning, and took him to a store in Easton owned by a Proslavery man. They set about organizing a kangaroo court to try Brown for murder. That was too slow for a bearded giant named Gibson—he smashed a hatchet into Brown's skull. Subdued by the act, the Rangers loaded their victim onto a wagon, drove him to his cabin, shouted "Here's Brown!" and dumped the frozen corpse onto the ground.

The bitter winter laid an icy moratorium upon the combatants. Most of the territory's settlers lived in log huts— floorless, one-room structures of poorly chinked, half-hewn logs, with doors and windows of cotton cloth. The wind blew fiercely through them, water froze in pitchers, families crouched in blankets near hearths, and it was not unusual to wake in the morning and find that snow had drifted in and covered the dirt floor to a depth of several inches. People in larger settlements fared little better. Politics and ideology were superfluous—life became a matter of pure animal survival.

Not so for the rest of the country, where shelter was more adequate and the climate not so severe. Congress was in turmoil, the old and new political parties were a

mishmash. Politicians came in every shape and size—
Whigs, Federalists, Democrats, Know-Nothings, old-line
Jeffersonian Republicans and the new Republicans who
were anathema to the South and who, because of their
abolitionist leanings, had been dubbed "Black Republicans." Kansas was the single common theme of the country, and how you felt about it depended upon which side
of the Mason-Dixon Line you lived.

If fiery newspaper articles had been lethal weapons, the
nation would have slaughtered itself in a month. Daily
appeals for money, men and arms were made from pul-
pits, legislative halls and business offices.

The most significant southern contribution to the war
effort came from Alabama. Major Jefferson Buford sold
40 slaves at $700 a head and used the proceeds to raise
and equip an army of 300 men. The day Buford's force
set out from Montgomery, a crowd of 5,000 turned out
to cheer them. A Baptist minister gave the major a large
Bible and said, "Providence may change our relations to
the inferior race, but the principle is eternal—the suprem-
acy of the white race." Colonel Zachabod Jackson from
Georgia also led a force to the Kansas Territory, as did
Colonel Warren D. Wilkes of South Carolina.

A proposal was made in the Georgia legislature to ap-
propriate $50,000 for the arming and equipping of mili-
tary companies. An emigrant aid bill was introduced in
the Alabama legislature—the proceeds to be gained by a
special tax on slave property in the state.

The North was not lagging behind. Committees were
raising money in most of the larger cities and people were
subscribing liberally to the New England Emigrant Aid

Society. Deacon Charles B. Lines of a New Haven congregation raised a contingent of seventy-nine Rifle Christians. These were supplied with Sharps rifles by a Brooklyn preacher named Henry Ward Beecher who called the rifles a greater moral agency in Kansas than Bibles. Sharps rifles were thereafter commonly referred to as Beecher's Bibles.

President Pierce was in trouble. Kansas was killing him politically. Secretary of War Jefferson Davis convinced the President that the only way to quiet things down was to admit Kansas to the Union as a state.

On January 24, 1856, Pierce asked Congress to pass an act enabling Kansas to frame a constitution. He endorsed the Proslave Territorial Legislature and condemned the formation of the Free Soil government and its defiance of the territorial government as revolutionary and an act of treason.

This designation was to be quite an important one.

But such an enabling act had to have northern support and the North had no intention of supporting it.

Congress muddled about. What to do about Kansas? What to do?

A dozen different bills were introduced—and defeated. Finally, agreement was reached. Congress, in all its wisdom and decisiveness, would send a three-man investigating committee to Kansas.

Meanwhile, Free Soilers were convinced that an all-out attack on Lawrence was imminent. They strengthened fortifications. They laid in provisions. They stockpiled gunpowder, lead and weapons, which were being shipped to them from the East.

Robinson and the committee of safety sent six men back East to raise an army. These set forth in the dead of winter, carrying with them various important documents. The problem was, how to cross Missouri without being apprehended? This was solved by donning rough border clothes and carrying liquor jugs, because, they reasoned, jugs were as much standard equipment for Missourians as were clothes. Whatever the truth of this intelligence, the ruse worked, and the ambassadors reached the Mississippi River, which was frozen solid, and walked across to Illinois, stopping midway to remove their papers, which were hidden in the jugs.

The Free State party convened again at Topeka on March 4. It passed a few laws, elected ex-Governor Reeder and Jim Lane provisional state senators and drew up a memorial asking admission to the Union under the Topeka Constitution. Then, after scheduling a meeting for July 4, it adjourned. Robinson had taken a cautious stand at the convention, so as to offer no provocation to either the Proslavery party or the federal government. Collision with either the central or the territorial government, he warned, was to be avoided.

Lane went off to Washington with the memorial and the constitution. What followed was a blow to Free Soil morale and an embarrassment to Lane, a man not easily embarrassed. Senator Lewis I. Cass of Michigan presented the documents to the Senate, where it was pointed out that, among other things, the memorial and constitution —full of addendums, erasures and crossouts, ragged and dirty—looked as if it had been written minute by minute during a heated discussion.

Senator Douglas noted that all the signatures had been written by the same hand.

Lane hastily withdrew the papers and had an affidavit sworn out claiming the original list of signatures had been lost and that Lane's private secretary had drawn up a new list. The affidavit also contained some apologetic mumbling about the appearance of the constitution and memorial. The Free Soil general persuaded Senator James Harlan of Iowa to submit it to the Senate a second time.

He fared no better. This time he was castigated for submitting an imperfect document, for having struck out (through shame) the indefensible and notorious Black Law. Douglas and a few others used the opportunity to assail Lane personally—and the grounds on which to assail him were many. But Lane didn't give up. He brought the documents to the House, which, after much argument, finally voted by a majority of two to admit Kansas. The Senate would have none of it and the bill was quashed. Lane went back to Kansas.

A congressional investigating committee arrived in Lawrence on April 17, set up headquarters at the Free State Hotel and began taking testimony from both sides.

Sam Wood, leader of the Branson rescue party, was back at Lawrence. The weather had improved somewhat and that ever-vigilant defender of Law and Order in Kansas Territory, Sheriff Jones, decided to open the political arrest season by picking up Mr. Wood. He rode into the Free Soil stronghold with three deputies.

Wood was on the street, but had no intention of being arrested. When he refused to come along, Jones grabbed him—and promptly received a punch in the mouth from another Free Soiler. A free-for-all began, and ended a few minutes later with Jones and his deputies having been disarmed and firmly trounced.

Jones left, but came back the next day, Sunday. This time a posse of ten rode with him. They spied Sam Tappan, another of the Branson rescuers, and went for him. Tappan was a decoy. A crowd of armed Free Soilers boiled out of a nearby church. While Jones gaped, Sam Tappan gave him his second punch in the mouth.

Jones rode to Lecompton, the new seat of the territorial government. There he detailed his grievances to Governor Shannon. Following the near disaster of the Wakarusa War, Shannon had been empowered by President Pierce to call out federal troops in cases of emergency. Governor Shannon decided that the foiled arrests and Jones's bruised jaw constituted an emergency.

On Wednesday, Jones and his deputy, Sam Salter, returned to Lawrence for the third time. Behind them rode a detachment of federal dragoons under the command of Lieutenant James McIntosh. It was a long day. The Free Soilers on Jones's list ducked from house to house, a few minutes ahead of the search party. No one in Lawrence, it seemed, was even *acquainted* with the offenders, let alone knew where they were. But Jones was persistent. By late afternoon he had arrested six men. Disappointingly, he had captured none of the ringleaders. The Law and Order force retired to its camp a little way out of town, at the edge of the river.

A crowd of Free Soilers gathered in the nearby woods that evening. There were angry grumblings and loud speculations as to the desirability of having a dead sheriff.

McIntosh and Jones were standing at a water barrel when a shot rang out. Jones said the shot was meant for him. The lieutenant shrugged it off as a scare round fired into the air. Jones showed the officer a bullet hole in his pants leg. McIntosh grew alarmed and went to talk with the Free Soilers.

While he was with them, another shot sounded in the darkness. A soldier rushed up and told the lieutenant that Sheriff Jones was dead.

The sheriff *had* been shot in the back, but was only wounded, far from dead. But rumor fanned out like a brush fire: *Sheriff Jones has been murdered by abolitionists!*

John Stringfellow's *Squatter Sovereign* screamed:

His murder shall be avenged, if at the sacrifice of every abolitionist in the Territory. We are now in favor of levelling Lawrence and chastising the traitors there congregated, should it result in the total destruction of the Union.

Lawrence knew it was in trouble. Free Soilers quickly passed a series of resolutions. The shooting, they said, was unexpected, undesired and unsupported by the community. The citizens of Lawrence deplored the act and offered Jones all the sympathy, aid and comfort in their power. They appointed five men to investigate the affair and ferret out the guilty party. They posted a five hundred dollar reward. Lawrencians were quite sincere in their repudiation of the deed and their attempts to find the man; although most would have been happy to see Jones carted to a graveyard, they were fully aware of the consequences his shooting might bring.

Whitfield, the Proslavery territorial delegate to Congress, was in Lawrence making a deposition to the House investigating committee at the time of Jones's shooting. He knew the massing evidence was not flattering to the Proslavery side. So, in the hopes of bogging down the investigation, he declared himself in fear of his life—saying it was unreasonable to expect the honest, law-loving Proslavery people of the territory to come into the assassins' den—and fled the town. His flight did not impede the committee at all, though, and he returned a few days later.

Whitfield was perfectly correct in assuming that the Proslavery side would not come out the hero. The committee's 1206-page report, issued some four months later, stated flatly that organized invasion from Missouri had carried the earlier elections and that the territorial legislature was an illegally constituted body having no power to pass valid laws. Their enactments, said the committee, were therefore null and void. This did the Free Soilers no tangible good, though, for Congress did not take any action.

In early May, the undauntable Reverend Pardee Butler, whom we last saw floating down the Missouri River on a pole-raft, returned to the town of Atchison, voicing his views on slavery. This time the Atchisonians wanted to hang him, and might have if an influential Missourian of venerable years had not called for a bit of restraint. The Atchisonians settled for tarring and feathering the reverend and running him out of town.

A grand jury was in session at Lecompton, under the direction of Samuel D. Lecompte, chief justice of the ter-

ritorial supreme court. In Judge Lecompte's charge to the
jury he insisted that the territorial legislature and its laws
were of United States authority and making and that all
those who "resist these laws resist the power and authority of the United States, and are therefore guilty of high
treason."

The grand jury promptly indicted ex-Governor Reeder,
James H. Lane, Charles Robinson and other Free Soilers
for high treason.

Further, they returned another indictment:

> . . . *The Herald of Freedom,* published at Lawrence, has
> from time to time issued publications of the most inflam-
> matory and seditious character, denying the legality of the
> territorial authorities, advising and commanding forcible
> resistance to the same . . . even to the extent of advising
> assassination as a last resort.

> Also, that the paper known as *The Kansas Free State* has
> been similarly engaged . . . and we respectfully recommend
> their abatement as a nuisance.

> Also . . . the "Free State hotel," in Lawrence . . . could
> only have been designed as a stronghold of resistance to
> law . . . and [we] respectfully recommend that steps be
> taken whereby this nuisance may be removed.

The Proslavery party was overjoyed—they now had
what they had lacked during the Wakarusa War: legal
grounds to move against Lawrence.

Reeder was subpoenaed to appear before the grand jury.
He refused the summons. When a deputy marshal went
to arrest him, Reeder, surrounded by a crowd of Free Soil-

ers, told the man it would be at his own peril. The lawman retired and Reeder fled from the territory.

Lane and Robinson also took flight. Robinson, though, was recognized and arrested in Lexington, Missouri. A United States Colonel named Preston was assigned to bring him back to Kansas. Their trip to Lecompton would take them through Lawrence, and Preston informed Robinson that he and his escort had been ordered to shoot the Free Soiler at once if any rescue attempt was made. Governor Shannon avoided that possibility by having Robinson jailed at Leavenworth instead of going on to Lecompton.

Confrontation was in the air.

Bands of Missourians and patrols of Buford's, Jackson's and Wilke's Southerners roamed through the territory. Free Soilers did not leave their settlements unless travel was absolutely essential. Deputy Sheriff Sam Salters issued passes to Proslavery partisans so they would not be harassed. With a flourish he wrote, "Let this man pass i no him two be a Law and abidin Sittisen."

On May 11, with indictments of the grand jury in hand, United States Marshal Israel B. Donaldson issued a proclamation calling for the law-abiding citizens of the territory to gather at Lecompton "in numbers sufficient for the execution of the law."

The proclamation circulated mainly in the territory's largest Proslavery settlements and widely through the Missouri border towns.

The people of Lawrence sent documents to Governor Shannon and to Marshal Donaldson denying the allegations of resistance made against them and reaffirming their willingness to submit to any judicial writs. They even offered to furnish the marshal a posse to help serve the writs. However, they stated bluntly that they would resist, to the death if need be, any invading mob.

The Proslavery forces began to gather at Lecompton. David Atchison came, leading his company of Platte County Rifles and bringing two pieces of artillery. The Kickapoo Rangers were there. John Stringfellow came with a force from the town of Atchison. Colonel Boone brought four hundred men from Westport. Buford's Alabamans gathered, and Wilkes's South Carolinans, and Titus's Floridians. Governor Shannon provided guns from the federal armory at Lecompton. Despite this, he later wrote to the President, "Had the Marshal called upon me for a posse, I should have felt bound to furnish him with one comprised entirely of United States troops."

Poised, much of the Proslavery army kept itself in supplies by looting the larders and livestock pens of Free Soil settlers.

Lawrencians tried desperately to avoid what they knew was coming. But Shannon wouldn't listen. Donaldson wouldn't listen. Colonel Sumner wouldn't listen. No one, it seemed, was interested.

And while Kansas Territory held its breath, Senator Charles Sumner (no relation to the Colonel) was wrathfully delivering one of the most blistering speeches ever heard in the United States Senate.

His philippic was entitled The Crime Against Kansas. He compared the actions of the Proslavery party to the worst betrayals and indignities of history. It was not even common lust for power, he thundered, but the rape of a virgin territory being compelled to the hateful embrace of slavery. It was the result of the depraved longing of the South for a new slave state. It was the crime of crimes, he stormed, a crime against nature itself from which the soul recoiled. He called the Missourians murderous robbers, hirelings picked from the drunken spew and vomit of an uneasy civilization. He called Senator Andrew Butler of South Carolina and Senator Douglas of Illinois the champions of human wrongs. Butler's passion for the harlot slavery, he said, surpassed even Don Quixote's for the harlot Dulcinea. Butler, who had led the defense of the Proslavery party in Kansas, discharged his incoherent phrases, said Sumner, in a flood of spittle, demonstrating a complete incapacity to speak the truth, disfiguring everything he touched.

The temper of Sumner's speech stunned even the perrenial Congressional firebrands.

It did more than stun House Representative Preston Brooks of South Carolina, a relative of Butler. Two days after the speech he stalked into the Senate Chamber carrying a gutta-percha cane one-inch in diameter. Brooks, a former cavalryman with combat experience, wielded the cane like a saber and brought it down hard across Sumner's head. Dazed and unable to rise from his desk there was little Sumner could do to defend himself. Brooks continued beating the senator until the cane broke, then pulled the butt up short and began his clubbing anew. When he was done he left Sumner sprawled unconscious and bleeding upon the floor.

Northern politicians and papers denounced the act as brutal and cowardly. Southern politicians and papers did not refer to Brooks without prefixing his name with either *gallant, courageous* or *noble.*

An attempt to have Brooks expelled from the House was soundly defeated—only one Southern representative voted for the motion. Admirers presented Brooks with several new and suitably inscribed canes.

Sumner's spinal column had been injured. He was treated by specialists in Boston, Washington and London, but was not able to resume senatorial duties regularly until December of 1859, three and a half years later.

In Kansas, the action against Lawrence began the same day Sumner fired the opening blasts of his speech. A young Free Soiler named Jones was carrying a bag of meal back to his home. He ran into one of Donaldson's patrols at Blanton's Bridge. They shot him down.

Three friends of Jones promptly rode out of Lawrence to avenge him. They engaged another patrol and one of them, Stewart, was killed in the exchange of fire.

The next day, May 20, Deputy Marshal Fain rode into Lawrence. This appeared to be a test. He made two arrests and took his prisoners out of town. Lawrencians offered no resistance; the deputy was not molested by so much as a shout. Lawrence sighed its relief when it saw no other sign of Donaldson's posse.

Short-lived relief—for on the morning of May 21 Free Soilers awoke to find the posse, eight hundred strong, drawn up in military companies on the side of Mt. Oread, which flanked the town. The Proslavery force had with them a battery of four cannons—their muzzles trained on Lawrence's business district. Lawrencians hastily evacuated their women and children to a nearby ravine, then settled fearfully to wait.

At eleven o'clock in the morning, Marshal Donaldson rode down the mountain in the company of ten unarmed men. According to their agreement, a number of prominent Free Soilers joined the marshal's party and assisted him in making three more arrests. Donaldson and his men dined at the Free State Hotel then left, with the bill unpaid.

The marshal carried back to Mt. Oread a letter from the Committee of Safety, pledging continued cooperation and asking protection under the national and territorial laws. He read the letter and addressed his army. He hereby dismissed them, he said, but he pointed out that Sheriff Jones had writs in his pocket and that anyone who wanted to was now free to join the sheriff's posse.

Jones appeared, still not fully recovered but able to ride. The Border Army cheered. Jones quickly selected twenty armed men as his guard and rode into Lawrence. There he met with Samuel C. Pomeroy and demanded all the Free Soilers' arms.

Pomeroy consulted with the Committee of Safety, then told the sheriff the Free Soilers were unwilling to surrender personal property. They would, though, turn over their cannon. Pomery led Jones to the secreted howitzer and a small number of Sharps rifles.

Jones was pleased. He now ordered the Free State Hotel evacuated. Free Soilers did not have to ask why. The sheriff's army was on the move down the mountain. Its vanguard, including the four cannons, had already entered town. Its banners whipped in the air—*The Suprem-*

acy of the White Race, South Carolina, Southern Rights,
Alabama for Kansas north of 36-30.

Ex-senator Atchison, according to later Free Soil accounts, had delivered a speech to the army less than an
hour ago and his words were still ringing in the Border
Ruffians' minds:

> Boys, this day I am a Kickapoo Ranger, by God! This
> day we have entered Lawrence with "Southern Rights" in-
> scribed upon our banner, and not one damned Abolitionist
> dared to fire a gun. Now, boys, this is the happiest day
> of my life. We have entered that damned town, and taught
> the damned Abolitionists a Southern lesson that they will
> remember until the day they die. And now, boys, we will
> go in again, with our high honorable Jones, and test the
> strength of that damned Free State Hotel, and teach the
> Emigrant Aid Company that Kansas shall be ours. Boys,
> ladies should, and I hope will, be respected by every gen-
> tleman. But when a woman takes upon herself the garb
> of a soldier by carrying a Sharps rifle, then she is no longer
> worthy of respect. Trample her under your feet as you would
> a snake! Come on, boys! Now do your duty to yourselves
> and your Southern friends. Your duty I know you will
> do. If one man or woman dare stand before you, blow
> them to hell with a chunk of cold lead.

The Proslavery *Squatter Sovereign* subsequently denied
this speech and claimed that, on the contrary, "He [Atchi-
son] exhorted the men above everything to remember
that they were marching to enforce, not to violate, laws;
to suppress, and not to spread, outrage and violence." But
this account seems doubtful at best, particularly in light of

Atchinson's behavior in Lawrence immediately afterwards.

The cannons were brought to bear on the Free State Hotel; then the posse splintered into wild, shouting groups. The first attack was on the offices of the *Free State.* The presses and furniture were demolished with axes and sledgehammers. Six months' stock of paper was tossed to the winds. Type cases were carried out and dumped into the river. A library of three hundred volumes was hacked to pieces with sabers. Broken books were impaled on bayonets and carried about as souvenirs. The *Herald of Freedom* suffered the same fate.

Then Atchison called for silence. When he had some semblance of what he wanted, he touched a burning taper to the breech of one of the cannons. The cannon roared.

But, embarrassingly, Atchison had missed the hotel.

The next thirty some shots, though, were accurate. However, they didn't do much more than punch holes in the concrete walls. The resourceful army planted two kegs of black powder in the basement and fired them. All this accomplished was the shaking down of some masonry and the shattering of the windows. Things were becoming frustrating. Piles of paper and broken furniture were brought from the printing offices, stacked inside the hotel and set afire. Within twenty minutes it was blazing nicely.

Sheriff Jones, like Atchison, informed the army that this was the happiest day of *his* life, then said: "I determined to make the fanatics bow before me in the dust and kiss the territorial laws. I have done it, by God! You are now dismissed. The orders of the court have been executed."

You are now dismissed was interpreted as *You now*

have free reign. The Proslavery army turned upon stores and private homes with joyous whoops. They stole money, clothing, arms, jewelry, anything that caught their fancy.

The last of them did not leave until dusk. They stopped long enough to plunder Charles Robinson's home on Mt. Oread; then they set fire to it and disappeared into the darkness, leaving the flames flickering brightly behind them.

The sack of Lawrence caused some regret and misgivings within a few of the Southern leaders. Even David Atchison was a little dubious. But later events indicated that the largest sorrow was caused by the Free Soilers' refusal to give the posse anything that remotely resembled a justification for the destruction and looting.

Most of the Proslavery party didn't lose any sleep over what they had done. That was too much to expect of men like, say, Stringfellow, who had sworn he was ready to kill even a baby if he knew it would grow up to be an abolitionist.

6.

THE POTTAWATOMIE MASSACRE

Free Soil spirits were at an all-time low. But back East the northern press was making great propagandistic hay from the sack of Lawrence. Could there now be any doubt, thousands of editorials asked, of the justness of the Free Soil cause and the opposing baseness and savagery of the Proslavery forces?

The answer, of course, was no—if you lived north of the Mason-Dixon Line.

Free Soilers had taken a beating, but they had not been crushed. Bands of looting, burning and murdering Southerners were roaming the territory at will. But equally determined bands of Free Soilers were also at work— like the eight guerrillas who ambushed eighteen Border Ruffians on the Santa Fe Trail, killed several and drove the rest off. And both sides were stealing horses in truly admirable, or, depending on your point of view, truly deplorable numbers.

The sack of Lawrence caused one man to take the first of a series of steps that eventually guaranteed him a permanent place in the hall of great American heroes—or villains.

He was John Brown, known in the Kansas Territory as Old Brown.

Brown's biographers have fought over him with the ferocity of alley cats: he was a saint, he was a cowardly horse thief; he was a great patriot, he was a traitor; he was the right arm of God, he was a gross murderer. In short, he was and still is the embodiment of all things good to those who love him, and the embodiment of all things evil to those who revile him.

It is not within the scope of this book to resolve the conflicts that surround this complex man. But a few basic facts can be presented here, and his role in the Kansas Territory is concrete fact, not speculation.

Old Brown arrived in Kansas in October 1855. He was fifty-five years old then, a man who had sired twenty children with two wives, a man whose life had been a series of bankruptcies and lawsuits, an inflexible, didactic and short-tempered man who had once said: "No political action will ever abolish the system of slavery. It will have to go out in blood. Those men who held slaves have even forfeited their right to live."

He came with his son-in-law, Henry Thompson. He came sitting straight-backed on the seat of a wagon loaded with firearms and heavy-bladed cutlasses.

John Brown came to Kansas—to fight not settle. He was a man of medium height who gave the impression of being taller. He was slender, clean-shaven and had a tight, grim mouth and cold blue-gray eyes. He believed, erroneously, that he was a direct descendant of the original

Mayflower Pilgrims. He had been reared in a strict Puritan tradition, the same tradition responsible for the witch trials of Salem. He was a man brimming with self-righteousness, who had believed from childhood that God intended him for great things. He found quotations in the Bible to justify and support this conviction. John Brown was God's Soldier, a Joshua and a Gideon of the Old Testament. His sense of justice was predicated upon the sword. He was an intense, troubled, ceaseless enemy of evil, merciless and intractable in his execution of God's will. His sovereign remedy was violence.

Months earlier Old Brown had sent five of his sons to Kansas Territory, and now, in response to their request for weapons and support, he came to their settlement at Osawatomie.

Free Soilers dominated this area and they practiced the general territorial habit of harassing local members of the opposition, driving them out by threat and when necessary by violent action. Old Brown was sorely disappointed when the Wakarusa War fizzled out. He had wanted a bloody confrontation then and there. He was convinced that the Free Soil leaders were cowards.

News of the attack upon Lawrence reached Osawatomie by courier on May 21. The Pottawatomie Rifles, a company under the command of John Brown, Jr., left for Lawrence that same afternoon. Old Brown was with them, commanding a smaller company of his own, which he kept apart from the Pottawatomie Rifles. A third Free Soil detachment joined them and the combined force marched through the night, stopping the next morning to make a temporary camp and to prepare breakfast.

A messenger arrived at this site and informed them that Lawrence had already been sacked. Old Brown was outraged. He spoke furiously about ridding the territory of Proslavery men once and for all. And he set his sons to sharpening cutlasses on a grindstone.

On the morning of May 23, Old Brown left camp to do murder. Some historians claim that he rode out upon receipt of news that Proslavery elements had taken advantage of the rifle companies' absence to menace the unprotected Free Soil families left behind. This, they say, is why Old Brown set out for Dutch Henry's crossing on the Pottawatomie River. Brown, however, took only seven men with him, four of them his sons. The rest of the Free Soil force moved on to Palmyra where it threatened Proslavery settlers until ordered to disperse two days later by a United States cavalry patrol. Had there been any reports of danger to their homes, they would have rushed back instead of pushing on to Palmyra.

John Brown's group consisted of his sons Owen, Frederick, Salmon and Oliver, his son-in-law Henry Thompson, and two men named Theodore Weiner and James Townsley. They all rode in Townsley's wagon, except Weiner who went on horseback.

Old Brown had not yet revealed his plans to them. En route to the Pottawatomie they met Free Soiler James Blood. Usually reserved, Brown chattered nervously with Blood, then cautioned him, "We are on a secret mission—don't speak of meeting us."

At nightfall the band made camp in a gulch a mile north of the Pottawatomie. Now Old Brown told them what he intended to do—kill the Proslavery men who lived on this stretch of the river. This would in turn cause all other southern sympathizers to pack up and leave in short order. Old Brown had a list of victims. Townsley balked. The idea was too much for his stomach.

Brown was not to be put off, but neither was Townsley easily convinced. The attacks were delayed twenty-four hours while Brown argued with Townsley. The old man hauled out his favorite text: "Without the shedding of blood, there can be no remission of sins." He mustered every argument he could think of and finally fell back on predestination: "I have no choice. It has been decreed by Almighty God, ordained from eternity, that I should make an example of these men." When Townsley feigned illness, Brown felt his pulse and said, "You are not sick, all you need is a smell of blood."

Eventually Brown made a concession that satisfied Townsley's scruples—he narrowed the death list down to six names.

The first attack was made at eleven o'clock on Saturday night, May 24. They approached the house of James Doyle, killed his dogs when the animals came snarling to drive them off, then hammered on the door and demanded Doyle's surrender in the name of the Northern Army. Having little choice, Doyle opened the door to them. Brown's party rushed in and ordered Doyle and his three sons—aged twenty-two, twenty and sixteen—to step outside with them. The Doyles were half dressed and unarmed; they could offer no resistance. Mrs. Doyle begged Old Brown to let her youngest boy remain. God's Avenger relented.

James Doyle and his two eldest sons accompanied the

raiders into the darkness. Moments later a single pistol shot sounded. Mrs. Doyle and her sixteen-year-old son sat together sleepless and terrified, until dawn. Then they went outside. They found James Doyle stabbed through the heart and shot in the forehead. The oldest boy's head was cleaved and he had been stabbed repeatedly in the side. The head of the younger boy had also been split open and his arms had been severed and his fingers had been cut from his hands.

Strangely, the single act of violence Old Brown himself committed that night was the firing of a shot into James Doyle's forehead, and he did that only after Doyle had been stabbed to death. No one has ever explained why he did not participate in the actual murders.

Brown's party left Doyle's and went to the home of Allen Wilkinson, a member of the territorial legislature. Again they banged on the door and identified themselves as the Northern Army. Wilkinson was awake, tending his wife who was sick with the measles. Their two small children were asleep in another bed.

Against his wife's pleading, Wilkinson opened the door. Four of the raiders entered the cabin and ordered the legislator outside. Mrs. Wilkinson begged them to let him stay; she needed him. "You've got neighbors," Old Brown said. "One of them can come." They told her they were taking him prisoner to their camp.

The next morning, Allen Wilkinson was found dead a hundred yards from his house, stabbed in the side, his skull split and his throat cut.

Old Brown's last visit of the night was to James Harris's home. Three guests were spending the night there—

William Sherman, John Whiteman and a third man whose name is not known.

Old Brown took Harris outside and questioned him in great detail about anti-Free Soil activities. Harris denied ever participating in any. Brown made him an offer: keep his mouth shut, leave the territory immediately, and he would not be harmed. Harris gave his word. William Sherman was then taken from the cabin. Sherman was the brother of Dutch Henry, a noted Proslavery man who was not home that evening and probably escaped death because of it. Sherman did not return.

Harris and Whiteman found his body the next morning lying in a creek next to the cabin. Sherman's skull had been split and some of his brains had been washed away by the water. He had been stabbed in the heart and one of his hands was attached to his wrist by only a thin strand of flesh.

It is unfortunate that the congressional investigating committee refused, with the exception of its minority member, to take evidence on the Pottawatomie Massacre. This decision added weight to the Proslavery charge that the committee had treated them unfairly. Although the widowed Mrs. Wilkinson and Mr. James Harris swore out affidavits against Brown, the old man neither denied nor admitted responsibility. He did say, though, that he approved of the murders. Any doubt concerning his role was eliminated years later when James Townsley confessed and Salmon Brown, who admitted killing one of the Doyle boys, gave a detailed account of the night's activities.

Free Soilers, although disturbed by the brutality, generally endorsed the killings. Samuel C. Pomeroy, who had not looked particularly courageous during the sack of Lawrence, said, "I don't care what are the consequences to me politically, I will, upon the first occasion, at the Capitol of this country—defend that old man who offered up himself gloriously—from the charge or crime of murder!" Charles Robinson compared Old Brown to Jesus Christ and said that Brown's actions at Pottawatomie had been a great service to the Free Soil cause.

Robinson reversed himself three years later when he was summoned to testify before a Congressional hearing on the Harpers Ferry raid. He there condemned the Pottawatomie Massacre, but the rest of the principal actors in the Kansas drama did not follow suit for another seventeen years—about the time they each began to scramble for the heroes' laurels.

The murders had two immediate effects. Some of the more faint-hearted Proslavery people packed up and left the territory at once. On the other hand, units of the army that had sacked Lawrence went to work on Free Soilers with a vengeance. At Leavenworth, the imprisoned Charles Robinson was nearly lynched by a mob.

Local residents of the Dutch Henry's Crossing area met, Free Soiler and Proslave together, and passed a joint resolution denouncing the murders. Free Soil participation in this resolution seems mostly motivated by a fear of reprisal.

Captain H. C. Pate, a Missourian who had led the Westport Sharpshooters against Lawrence, was still in the territory. News of the massacre reached him at Franklin and he rode immediately with his fifty men to Osawatomie to hunt for Old Brown. But the only Browns the Sharpshooters could find were the old man's sons, Jason and John Jr. The Missourians took the two boys prisoner and set fire to John Jr.'s house along with Theodore Weiner's store. The company headed north, then, in the direction Old Brown was rumored to be moving. They carried the Brown boys with them, the youths in chains and made to walk. John Jr. broke under the strain, pulled and tore at his chains and raved like a wild man. Pate's force encountered a federal cavalry patrol some twenty-five miles later and turned their prisoners over to the soldiers, who took the boys to Lecompton.

On Saturday, May 31, the Border Ruffians made camp at the head of Black Jack ravine, five miles east of Palmyra. A small party rode into Palmyra that evening, looted homes and stores and brought back two prisoners. One of their captives was a Baptist minister named Moore, a temperance preacher. Pate's company amused itself by jamming a funnel into the man's mouth and pouring whiskey down his throat until he was staggering and sick.

On Sunday afternoon half a dozen Sharpshooters mounted up and rode into Prairie City for a repeat performance of their Palmyra spree. A circuit preacher was holding services in one of Prairie City's larger cabins. This was most unfortunate for the raiders, since the congregation that day included two dozen Free Soil men who, notwithstanding the homage they had come to pay the Lord, had brought their guns along.

Someone sounded the alarm as the Missourians approached. The Free Soilers rushed outside. There was a quick rattle of musketry. A moment later two of the raiders lay dead in the dirt and the remaining four were riding for their lives.

Five days earlier, while Pate and his Missourians were galloping to Osawatomie from Franklin, Old Brown led his murder party to the head waters of Ottawa Creek to confront two small parties of Border Ruffians rumored to be searching for them. He found none in the immediate area, so he made camp to see what would develop next.

On May 31, while Pate's men were looting Palmyra Captain S. T. Shore of the Prairie City Rifles visited Brown's camp and told him that a large body of Missourians was now camped at Black Jack. Old Brown and Shore decided to attack.

The Prairie City Rifles, eighteen strong, joined the Brown party. Couriers were sent to Palmyra and to Captain Abbott's Blue Mound Infantry which was camped on the Wakarusa. The Free Soil force numbering a little less than thirty arrived at a grove two miles west of Black Jack at midnight, on Monday, and drew battle plans.

Free Soilers took up positions on the summit of a hill overlooking Pate's camp at dawn Tuesday morning. Old Brown gave the signal and the attack began. Brown's party, armed with muskets, raced down the slope to gain a better firing range, while Shore's company blazed away from the summit with their more accurate and longer-carrying Sharps rifles.

The engagement went on for three hours. Some of the Missourians, fearing the momentary arrival of Free Soil reinforcements, began to slip away from their captain. When Brown's men concentrated their fire on the Missourians' mounts and killed four of them, the Border Ruffians' desertion rate rose sharply; without horses, later escape would be impossible.

The battle ended when Old Brown's half-wit son Frederick came charging up on horseback waving a cutlass and yelling to his father that the Missourians were surrounded. Pate, thinking reinforcements had arrived, surrendered.

Twenty-three of the Missourians were left, eight of them wounded. The Free Soilers captured their arms and provisions and recovered four wagonloads of plunder. Free Soil casualties were not recorded, but it is known that Henry Thompson was shot through the lungs.

Captain James Abbott arrived with his men shortly after the surrender, and by the end of the day Captain Samuel Walker's Bloomington Rifles, Captain Joseph Cracklin's Lawrence Stubbs and Captain McWhinney's Wakarusa Boys had also ridden in, swelling the Free Soil force to one hundred fifty men.

An army of three hundred Missourians was also in the area, under command of Whitfield, the territorial delegate. It had taken the field after the Pottawatomie Massacre, planning to link up with Pate and then, with the consolidated force, sweep every abolitionist from the area.

The two armies were now within striking distance of each other, poised and waiting.

But Colonel Sumner suddenly arrived with fifty dragoons and a proclamation issued by Governor Shannon on the previous day ordering all armed and illegal organizations to disband and disperse.

Sumner and his soldiers visited the Free Soil camp first.

The colonel said he had come to release Pate and his men and to aid Deputy Marshal Fain in the arrest of John Brown. It was quickly discovered, though, that Fain had lost his warrant. Sumner ruled that without the warrant, no arrest could be made.

Captain Pate thundered his indignation, but Sumner told him, "I don't want to hear a word out of you, sir. Not a word, sir. You have no business here. The governor told me so."

The Free Soilers left the field. Old Brown and his party returned to their homes, free men, happy in the knowledge that they had struck a blow for God and freedom.

Sumner and his troop then rode to Whitfield's camp, where the Missourians agreed to break up and return to their homes as ordered. A portion of them went by way of Osawatomie, pillaged the town and turned three Free Soilers into corpses.

7.

FREE SOILERS
ON THE OFFENSIVE

There was a hurricane blowing in the East, and it was named General James H. Lane. The flamboyant Free Soiler was raging and stomping, begging and pleading and roaring before huge rallies, sweeping up his listeners like so many dry leaves and doing with them what he willed. What he willed, of course, was to squeeze every possible ounce of support from them that could be had. Other Free Soil men were speaking in the North, too, but none could bring an entire audience leaping to its feet, shouting its loyalty and shelling out money by the handful.

Lane's "Bleeding Kansas" speech became nearly as famous and as cherished in the North as the Bill of Rights. State legislatures passed resolutions expressing solidarity with Kansas Free Soilers and pledged financial and material aid. Various state aid societies welded together into the National Kansas Committee and raised nearly a quarter of a million dollars for arms, supplies and settler support. Groups of men determined to hold Kansas for the North left major cities daily.

Lane's most spectacular triumph was in Chicago on May 31. The crowd was so immense that Lane moved them from the Metropolitan Opera Hall into the open air where he addressed them from the steps of the courthouse. He detailed all the outrages committed by the "slavocracy," and several more that had occurred only in his imagination. He modestly reminded them of his own heroic war record in Mexico, then said with feigned amazement, "It did not occur to me [then] that I should be indicted for treason because I loved liberty better than slavery." He went on to quote from the territorial laws: "To kidnap a white child into slavery, six months in jail —to kidnap a nigger into freedom, death!" Finishing, he worked his audience to a fever pitch, then flung out his arms and shouted, "Now, before God, and his people, I arraign Frank Pierce as a murderer!" When he called for contributions, Chicagoans surged forward and emptied their pockets.

As the Grim Chieftain continued his speaking tour, the idea of Lane's Army of the North sprang up. The South grew hysterical. Its newspapers screamed warnings. Invasion by a large, well-armed horde of abolitionists was imminent. Northern papers also picked up the idea. The *New York Weekly Times* reported Lane to be at Council Bluffs with an army of one thousand bloodthirsty buffalo hunters, all eager to overrun and take control of Kansas.

This year, 1856, was an election year and the national parties were hammering out platforms and choosing their candidates. Slavery was the only real issue, and Kansas was the key. The Democrats convened in Cincinnati. "Unionism" was their catchword and the only way to preserve the Union, they said, was to stand by the Kansas-

Nebraska Bill and let territories decide for themselves whether or not they would have slaves. The party dumped the rather ineffectual Pierce, passed over Stephen Douglas, and nominated James Buchanan.

The Republicans assembled in Philadelphia. Their word was "Freedom," and they demanded that Congress prohibit slavery in the territories. General John C. Frémont, known as the Pathfinder for his exploration of the West, was their nominee.

The fragments of disintegrating parties, mostly Whigs and Know-Nothings, also met in Philadelphia, calling themselves the American party. They were the "Americans must rule America" group—antiforeigners. And they felt that both Congress and individual states should leave the territories and each other alone. Their man was Millard Fillmore.

While the country was snarling, barking and growling at itself, settlers from both North and South, but mainly from the North, were streaming into Kansas. Free Soilers were still staggering from the blows they had taken, but they managed to pull themselves together and prepare for their Fourth of July Convention and the opening of the Free State Legislature at Topeka.

Governor Wilson Shannon, however, had other ideas. Late in June, he ordered Colonel Sumner to prevent the Free Soil Legislature from meeting. Then, feeling that discretion was indeed the better part of valor, he promptly left the territory.

The Fourth of July was scorching, one hundred degrees in the shade. But Free Soilers flocked to Topeka, and a gala festival complete with fireworks and a band began in the early morning. Several companies of Free State Militia performed military drill for the holiday crowd, then assembled to receive banners from a delegation of women: OUR LIVES FOR OUR RIGHTS.

Shortly before noon, Colonel Sumner rode into town at the head of two hundred cavalrymen. He brought a battery of light artillery with him. The colonel snapped out orders; the soldiers dismounted and took up positions. Two cannons were wheeled into place and cannoneers stood by with slow matches in hand.

Sumner strode into the assembly hall. He said to the gathering legislature:

Gentlemen, I am called upon this day to perform the most painful duty of my whole life. Under the authority of the President's proclamation, I am here to disperse this Legislature, and therefore inform you that you cannot meet. I therefore order you to disperse. God knows that I have no party feeling in this matter, and will hold none so long as I occupy my present position in Kansas. I have just returned from the borders where I have been sending home companies of Missourians, and now I am ordered here to disperse you. Such are my orders, and you must disperse. I now command you to disperse. I repeat that it is the most painful duty of my whole life.

He would, he said when questioned, use all the forces under his command to carry out his orders. He left the assembly hall and addressed the waiting crowd, assuring them he had no wish to interfere with their celebration and that now, having done his duty, he would leave. The troopers remounted and as they filed out of town the Free

Soilers gave three cheers for Colonel Sumner, three more for John Frémont and three groans for Franklin Pierce.

Missourians were determined to blockade Kansas. They set up a series of checkpoints along the Missouri River complete with artillery emplacements. They overhauled steamboats, seized consignments of Free State merchandise, appropriated weapons, arrested those emigrants who could not give good accounts of themselves and turned back hundreds more. Their largest prize was a shipment of Sharps rifles valued at four thousand dollars and destined for Free Soil forces in Lawrence. Overland routes were also policed, wagons searched and parties with only a few women among them were automatically turned back.

Seventy-five Chicagoans who had been recruited after Lane's speech in that city were stopped at Lexington and relieved of their Sharps rifles. They were subjected to a second search at Leavenworth and stripped of "about two bushels of revolvers, pistols, and bowie-knives," then sent back downriver and put ashore at the Illinois border during a thunderstorm and left to shift for themselves.

The *Squatter Sovereign* found the search and seizure method too tame. Its editors wrote:

> We are of the opinion that if the citizens of Leavenworth would hang one or two boat-loads of abolitionists it would do more towards establishing peace in Kansas than all the speeches that have been delivered in Congress during the present session. Let the experiment be tried!

There were no hangings, but Captain Emory's Leavenworth Regulators did round up several dozen Free Soilers and send them packing down the river. And William Philips, the Free Soil lawyer who had been tarred, feathered and sold by a slave, was murdered.

Predatory guerrilla warfare became a way of life with each side murdering and looting. Farmers worked their fields armed and in groups of five and ten. When strangers met, hands drifted toward weapons and the introductory question was "Free Soil or Slave?"

The thwarted Chicago contingent linked up with emigrants from several other states, to a total of nearly four hundred, and tried again, this time by one of the Iowa-Nebraska routes that effectively flanked the Missouri blockade. General James H. Lane was riding with them.

The National Kansas Committee was jittery. Rumors about Lane caused them to investigate the Free Soiler. What they discovered frightened them. They wanted Kansas for the North, yes, but by peaceful settlement. So they sent a message requesting Lane to disassociate himself from the emigrant party.

In Missouri and in the territory it was believed that the group was merely the advance guard of Lane's apocryphal Army of the North. The Free Soil majority, still leaderless, was unwilling to set aside its tactic of passive resistance. Captain Samuel Walker was selected to ride to Lane and dissuade him from bringing his army into the territory.

Walker was a militant abolitionist, a small scrappy man who walked with a limp. Whatever tolerance he might have felt toward the Proslavery faction was smashed when a Proslavery preacher refused to let Walker's seriously injured daughter be carried into his house. Walker was strongly loyal to Lane and considered himself the Grim Chieftain's friend. It was felt that Lane would listen to him.

Nobody realized yet that Lane never listened to anyone but himself.

On his way north, Walker overtook and merged with a small party captained by Old Brown, who was determined to meet Lane's army and lead it back to victory or death. They located Lane and his convoy just outside Nebraska City. If it truly was an army, then the world has rarely seen a sorrier one. Its members were forlorn, tattered, broke and had nearly exhausted their supplies.

Walker found Lane close to tears. The general had just received the National Committee's request. Gently, Walker informed him of the Free Soil sentiment in the territory. Always on the alert for melodrama, Lane bowed his head, then said, "Walker, if you say the people of Kansas don't want me, it's all right. I'll cut my throat today."

But refraining a while from unsheathing his knife, he allowed himself to be coaxed from his disconsolate mood. A short time later, disguised as a Captain Joe Cook, he set off with Walker, Old Brown and a few others for the territory. It was an exhausting ride: they covered 150 miles in thirty hours. Weary men and animals dropped out along the way. Lane arrived in Lawrence alone at three o'clock in the morning, having interrupted his journey only for a few minutes in Topeka—long enough to dash off a florid note to the treason prisoners in Lecompton, announcing the triumphant arrival of his Army of the North and offering to attack the federal troops and free them.

Lawrencians quickly apprised him of the local situation. In addition to the Missouri blockades and increasing general harassment, three Proslave forts had been erected —at Franklin, Saunders and on Colonel Titus's land. Free Soil supplies were not being permitted to reach Lawrence. This was clearly intolerable. And for Lane there was only one solution to an intolerable situation—action. And so he marched with eighty-six men against Franklin.

The fort consisted of a strong blockhouse flanked on one side by a hotel and on the other by a post office. The Free Soilers advanced, fired a single volley, then called upon the garrison to surrender. They were answered by gunshots. The attack lasted three hours, both sides firing heavily. Finally, the Free Soilers set fire to a wagonload of hay and rolled it up against the fort. The defenders came boiling out and victory was Lane's. It was discovered that not a single man had been killed on either side, which was an embarrassing commentary on the day's marksmanship.

Lane announced that this attack represented a turning-point. Free Soilers, he said, would no longer follow a line of nonresistance. As an example, he was going to execute Sam Crane, the Franklin postmaster. But when Crane's wife interceded, Lane relented. The Free Soilers looted the fort and brought the spoils back to Lawrence. Their chief prize was Old Sacramento, a cannon that had been hauled hundreds of miles through the desert during the Mexican War by the men of the famous colonel from Missouri, Alexander W. Doniphan.

Lane claimed the fall of Fort Franklin as the first

victory for his Army of the North, though not a single emigrant who had made the trek with him had been present at the attack. The Proslavery faction, however, did not know this, and it was widely believed that Lane's bloodthirsty horde had indeed arrived.

Fort Saunders, southwest of Lawrence, was the next target. It was an impressive fortification—1,375 square feet, and two stories high, with thick walls and rows of rifle loopholes. It was estimated that a garrison of one hundred men could stand off an attack by a thousand. Free Soil Major David S. Hoyt volunteered to learn the number of defenders. He entered Fort Saunders if not in a friendly way, then at least peacefullly, possibly under a white flag. Free Soilers later found his corpse a little ways from the fort. Two bullets had passed through his body, and a third, a *coup de grâce,* through his head.

Colonel James A. Harvey arrived in Lawrence the day Hoyt's murder was reported. Harvey and a small company of Chicagoans had been with the emigrant party in Nebraska, and if anyone qualified as members of Lane's Army of the North, it was Harvey and his men. They were mostly a rough, rootless bunch, and, like their twenty-nine-year-old colonel, who had left a wife and daughter behind, they had come to Kansas for action, not agriculture. Searching federal troops had not discovered the arms cache hidden beneath their seedbags. Hearing that Lane and Old Brown were massing men for an attack on Fort Saunders, Harvey and his company rode out of town to join.

Harvey favored immediate assault, but Lane wanted a chance to exercise his oratorical skills and to gather more men. So Hoyt's body was put on display, and Lane, with moist eyes and quavering voice, drew more and more volunteers until the Free Soil force numbered five hundred.

One report claims Lane had each man make a straw dummy, so that when men and dummies were loaded into wagons, the Free Soilers appeared to be twice their actual number. Whatever the truth of this, the garrison of Fort Saunders *did* count the approaching army at twelve hundred heads, and they promptly abandoned the fort. Free Soilers took the stronghold, gained a sizeable amount of arms, powder and supplies, but had been denied the satisfaction of a battle. Lane tried to make it up to them with a speech, then he turned command over to Sam Walker and made one of his characteristically mysterious exits. When next heard from, he was in Nebraska.

Walker wanted to return to his home, so he dismissed the brigade. Many men followed his example, but an equal number remained in company formation and rode off looking for trouble.

Early the next morning, the Topeka-Lecompton-Lawrence stage stopped in front of Walker's cabin. The driver called the captain out and informed him in a hushed voice: "I've got Titus's wife and two children in the stage. If you want to get the damned scoundrel, now is your time."

Walker and Major Henry Titus had a long history of enmity. Their homes were only three miles apart and earlier in the summer. Titus had led Proslavery men in a night raid on Walker's cabin. But Walker had advance warning and when the night riders arrived, thirty Free

Soilers in Walker's cabin blazed away at them from rifle slits cut into the walls and drove them off.

The next day Titus offered a reward of three hundred dollars for Sam Walker's head "on or off his shoulders." A few weeks later, with Walker still in possession of his head, Titus upped the prize to five hundred dollars.

Walker found the idea of an attack quite acceptable. He sent a runner to Lawrence, ordering Old Sacramento brought down; then he rounded up the few dozen men he could find and headed for Fort Titus. En route they encountered Harvey and his troop. The Chicagoans had killed one of Titus's men in a night skirmish and were eager to have a go at the stronghold. Old Brown, with his uncanny sense of finding the right spot at the right time, also appeared with a few of his sons and joined Walker's party.

Dark storm clouds rumbled while the Free Soilers deployed themselves around the complex of buildings that was Titus's estate. At Walker's signal, they opened fire. The many Southerners encamped in tents and in the sheds grabbed their rifles and raced to Titus's blockhouse. The attack continued several hours, with a good number of casualties on both sides, but seemed to be a stand-off. Walker himself had been knocked down by a shotgun blast and had taken several pieces of buckshot in the chest. But the lead had not gone deep and he retained command.

Finally, Old Sacramento appeared. The cannon was aimed point blank at the blockhouse. *Herald of Freedom* type salvaged from the river had been melted into balls and these were what the Free Soilers used to pound holes into the blockhouse. When the Proslavery men still did not surrender, a wagonload of burning hay was rolled up against the walls. Minutes later, the white flag went up.

The storm broke as the beaten Proslavery men trooped out. Rain drenched them. There were twenty-seven disheveled men—six more were in the blockhouse, too badly wounded to move.

Titus appeared in the doorway, grimy, slumpshouldered, stained with blood from three wounds. Walker relieved the major of his sword, saying, "Well, Titus, I beat you to it." He cocked his pistol and aimed at the Southerner's head.

But as fierce a partisan as Sam Walker was, he could not murder a man in cold blood. As the Free Soiler told it later, "The cuss got me in the right place. He saw the devil was to pay and he made a personal appeal to me. 'You have children, so have I,' he pleaded. 'For God's sake, save my life.'"

Titus's estate was plundered. Harvey's men appropriated all the tents for their own use. The major's pillared mansion was set to the torch; no one knew until later that there was a badly wounded man on the second floor who burned to death in the blaze. A Free Soiler recorded the words of one of Titus's slaves who laughed hilariously as he watched the mansion burn: "Masa Titus wanted six abolitionists for breakfast! Yah! Yah! Gorra Massy! guess he get his belly full dis mo'nin'."

The captured Proslavery men were brought to Lawrence. Three forts in five days! Free Soilers were jubilant. Governor Wilson Shannon was terrified. He came to Lawrence on August 17, the day after Fort Titus fell. To hint at the power behind him, he brought along Major John Sedgwick of the United States Cavalry. Peace, Shannon insisted, there must be peace. He spent most of the day in conference with the available Free Soil leaders.

A treaty was drawn. Its terms were simple: each side would free its prisoners, Old Sacramento would be sent back to Lecompton, and the Free Soil cannon removed from Lawrence in May would be returned.

Shannon then went outside to address the citizens. But this was a new, tough Lawrence, thronging with arrogant, aggressive men who had come in over the Lane Trail, as the Iowa-Nebraska route was called. They waved guns and shouted the governor down. Samuel Walker, possessed of a strong sense of frontier ethics, leaped upon his horse with drawn pistols and shouted that only over his dead body would the governor be insulted. Nobody, it seemed, wished to insult the governor that much.

With the treaty in hand and at least some semblance of peace restored, Shannon returned to Lecompton. Upon his arrival, he wrote to General Pulsifer Smith, who had replaced Colonel Sumner:

> We are threatened with utter extermination by a large force of free-state men. I have just returned from Lawrence, where I have been this day with a view to procuring the release of nineteen prisoners that were taken. I saw in that place at least 800 men who manifested a fixed purpose of destroying this town.

One day later, on August 18, he sat down at his desk again. This time he wrote to President Franklin Pierce. His letter was a resignation.

The Kansas-Nebraska Act of 1854, which permitted those territories to decide for themselves whether they were to be slave or free, was largely the work of Illinois Senator Stephen A. Douglas.

Missouri Senator David R. Atchison upheld the southern point of view in his strong opposition to the Act.

Border Ruffians from Missouri crossed over into Kansas Territory to prevent its becoming a free state.

Dr. Charles Robinson, a leader of the New England Emigrant Aid Society, played a major role in the Free Soil cause. He later became the first governor of Kansas.

Thousands of Missourians cast illegal votes in the Kansas Territory election of 1855. As a result, the new territorial legislature was overwhelmingly Proslavery.

Lawrence, Kansas, founded by the Aid Society, was a collection of crude cabins in 1854.

James H. Lane was one of the dominant figures in the history of Kansas Territory and a major advocate of the Free Soil cause.

Governor Wilson Shannon, a weak man, had little success in keeping peace between Free Soil and Proslavery factions.

Troops from as far away as South Carolina joined Proslavery forces in Missouri.

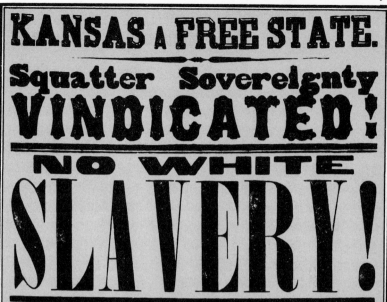

Broadsides such as this one rallied Free Soil Kansans to meet the threat from Missouri.

The residents of Lawrence were forced to surrender their single cannon to an army of Border Ruffians in 1856.

The Proslavery army then proceeded to destroy Lawrence's Free-State Hotel. Ex-Senator Atchison fired the first cannon shot, but missed the hotel.

John Brown, sometimes known as Old Brown, was a rabid Abolitionist. He and his sons were responsible for the infamous Pottawatomie Massacre.

On orders from Governor Shannon, Colonel E. V. Sumner dispersed the Free-State Legislature on July 4, 1856.

James Montgomery led the Jayhawkers, a group of Free Soilers known for its violent tactics.

Proslavers countered Jayhawker depredations with the Marais des Cygnes Massacre, in which five Free Soilers were killed and five wounded.

Jayhawkers often crossed the border into Missouri to steal horses and commit other outrages.

This party rescued Dr. John Doy from Missouri after he had been arrested illegally while conducting a group of free blacks out of Kansas.

8.

IT LOOKS LIKE — PEACE?

Proslavery forces did not stand idle while Free Soilers were capturing the forts around Lawrence. Marauding bands of Southerners were burning and plundering Free Soil homes throughout the territory, driving immigrants out in sizeable numbers. Ex-Senator Atchison and the Proslavery junta delivered an address in which they claimed civil war had been declared and begged all friends of law and order to rally to the cause. In Leavenworth, a Border Ruffian bet six dollars against a pair of boots that he could scalp an abolitionist within two hours. He won his boots.

Raid and counterraid was the order of the day.

Daniel Woodson, a young Marylander, was the territory's secretary of state and as such he became acting governor upon Shannon's resignation. When Woodson assumed the gubernatorial chair on August 21 the Proslavery party was jubilant. As General Pulsifer Smith put it, "If Mr. Atchison and his party had had the direction of affairs, they could not have ordered them more to suit their purpose." Four days after taking control, Woodson issued a proclamation in which he declared the territory in a state of open insurrection and rebellion. He called upon all patriotic citizens to come forth, defend the law and punish the traitors. Missouri pamphleteers threw their weight behind the call, pointing out that so long as Woodson was in power, the South had a clear field. They couldn't afford to miss the chance; the next governor might be an idiot.

The proclamation brought Atchison back into the territory, leading twelve hundred men. They made camp on Bull Creek, fifteen miles north of Osawatomie. General John Reid led two hundred fifty of these Missourians against Osawatomie the next morning. Reverend Martin White rode with them, a rabid Proslavery preacher who had been driven from this area by Free Soilers a few weeks earlier. On the way to Osawatomie, the raiders met Old Brown's half-wit son Frederick. Reverend White recognized him and fired, killing the boy instantly. "The ball passed clean through his body," the minister used to say with pride.

Free Soil scouts sounded an alarm, but most of the northern partisans were out menacing Proslave settlements and only forty-one men could be raised for the town's defense. Old Brown took command and deployed them in the woods and thickets along the Marais des Cygnes River. They opened fire when the Missourians rode into range. Reid's force dismounted, fanned out and returned fire. Then the Southerners unlimbered a six-pound cannon and blasted grapeshot at the Free Soilers, most of which passed harmlessly overhead. The outnumbered Free Soilers fled after a short battle, having killed four or five of the Missourians and leaving behind six of their own dead. Reid and his men moved on to the town.

When they left a short time later, only four cabins were still standing.

Lane returned suddenly from Nebraska. He gathered up men from Topeka and Lawrence and marched against ex-Senator Atchison with an army of three hundred. The two forces surveyed each other, jockeyed for position, fired a few volleys, then inexplicably withdrew—Atchison toward Missouri and Lane toward Lawrence.

Woodson was riding high and Free Soilers were being arrested, beaten and burned out by the dozens. The acting-governor ordered Colonel Cooke to march against Topeka, confiscate all arms, make prisoners of the insurrectionists and level all breastworks and fortifications. Cooke prudently refused and was backed up by his commanding officer, General Pulsifer Smith. The citizens of Lecompton were less restrained. Led by the honorable Sheriff Jones they burned down every Free Soil home in town.

Lane, upon hearing this news, decided to devastate Lecompton. He sent Colonel James A. Harvey with one hundred fifty men a little north of Lecompton to cut off the Proslavery line of retreat, then marched from the south with three hundred men and two artillery pieces. They might well have razed the town had their timing been more accurate.

Harvey's force arrived in the evening of September 4 and lay all night on the ground soaked by a cold drizzle, listening vainly for gunfire. In the morning Harvey concluded with disgust that the expedition had been abandoned, and he returned to Lawrence.

Lane had delayed his march nearly twenty-four hours.

The citizens of Lecompton learned of the impending assault and appealed to Colonel Cooke for help. The colonel rode out with a force of dragoons and intercepted Lane's advance guard a mile from Lecompton. When Lane sighted the soldiers, he jumped from his horse, grabbed a musket and melted into the ranks. Samuel Walker claimed command. Cooke parlayed with him and other captains. In the middle of the conference a United States deputy marshal appeared and demanded the arrest of Walker and Lane. Lane, Cooke told him, was not there, and as for arresting Walker the deputy could go to hell. Cooke was having enough trouble trying to calm things as it was.

Cooke argued eloquently. He pointed out that the Missourians were leaving the field, that the President had promised to release the political prisoners at Lecompton and that things in general were going well for the Free Soilers. After some reflection, Walker agreed to retire.

President Pierce was alarmed by the fresh outbreaks of violence in Kansas. And his alarm was heightened by editorials in southern newspapers screaming that Kansas was now in a state of open civil war. One wrote that every true Southerner should hurry there at once, bringing "a double-barrel gun, a brace of Colts revolvers and a trusty knife." Numerous reports placed Lane at the head of three thousand lawless abolitionists massed on the territory's border ready to give bloody answer to Acting-Governor Woodson, who had said, "Let the watchword be extermination total and complete."

Pierce dropped his other duties and hunted frantically for a new governor—one strong enough to rule this warring territory. He picked John W. Geary. It was a good choice. Geary was an impressive six-and-a-half foot Pennsylvanian who had fought in the Mexican War and, as the first mayor of San Francisco, had dealt successfully with border outlaws and vigilance committees. Pierce promised Geary full cooperation of the Army and, to help relax the tension, ordered the release of Robinson and other prisoners—at least on bail until they could be duly tried.

Geary came steaming up the Missouri River a few days after Lane's army had been turned back from Lecompton. His boat, the *Keystone,* docked at Glasgow on September 7. A huge crowd was milling on the dock, including a company of Border Ruffians recruited by Captain Claiborne Jackson. Dr. John W. Gihon, Geary's personal secretary, wrote: "Each man carried some description of fire-arm, not any two of which were alike. There were muskets, carbines, rifles, shotguns, and pistols of every size, quality, shape, and style." There were also a cannon and several ammunition wagons. Gihon moved among the Ruffians as they boarded and he discovered that, "The most they seemed to understand was that they were to receive so much per diem for going to Kansas to hunt and kill abolitionists."

It happened that Ex-Governor Shannon's eastbound boat was also docked at Glasgow. Geary and Shannon held a short conversation in which Shannon painted a grim picture, claiming rampant murder and roads filled with the bodies of slaughtered men.

The boat moved upriver and Geary saw war preparations in town after town. At Kansas City a wagon stood hitched near the pier. The name *Border Ruffian* was painted in flaming capitals on its side. There were large numbers of raiders lounging along the levee. Gihon wrote:

> Imagine a man standing in a pair of long boots, covered with dust and mud and drawn over his trousers, the latter made of coarse, fancy-colored cloth, well soiled; the handle of a large Bowie knife projecting from one or both boottops; a leather belt buckled around his waist, on each side of which is fastened a large revolver; a red or blue shirt, with a heart, anchor, eagle, or some other favorite device braided on the breast and back, over which is swung a rifle or carbine; a sword dangling by his side; an old slouched hat, with a cockade or brass star on the front or side, and a chicken, turkey, or goose feather sticking in the top; hair uncut and uncombed, covering his neck and shoulders; an unshaven face and unwashed hands.

A band of these men boarded the ship and searched for abolitionists.

Geary reached Leavenworth on September 9. He found a town barricaded against an expected attack by Lane and his Army of the North, a town swarming with armed whiskey-guzzling men who roared laughter as they explained to each other just what they were going to do with the abolitionists. It was a town completely under military rule. The governor continued up to Fort Leavenworth, where he discussed the situation with General Smith. The fort was jammed with Free Soil refugees seeking protection from Captain Emory's Leavenworth Regulators. Somber, Geary left the next morning for Lecompton.

He found the citizens of the capital also preparing to fend off an attack by Lane. Geary knuckled down to work immediately and made his position clear. He wanted peace in Kansas Territory and he meant to have it. He supported the concept of popular sovereignty, but he was determined to stop all interference by nonresidents. He demanded that the territorial laws be upheld, but he pledged his administration to the removal of all discriminatory laws against members of any given political persuasion. He issued two proclamations—the first disbanding the present volunteer "militia" now in the field, the second creating a new militia to be composed of Free Soilers as well as Proslavery men.

He saw to it that Robinson and the others were released on bail and he petitioned Washington for the removal of Proslavery Judge Lecompte, Indian Agent General Clarke and Marshal Donaldson.

John W. Geary was taking over, and he wanted no doubts of that fact in anyone's mind.

Instantly there was trouble. Harvey and his men had left Lawrence to fight a Proslavery force farther north. Lane was en route to Nebraska. Now the nearly defenseless Lawrencians informed Geary that a Missouri army of three thousand was marching on their town. They begged his protection. Outraged, Geary ordered Colonel Cooke into the saddle along with four hundred dragoons. A battery of light artillery was also moved out. Geary arrived in Lawrence at dawn.

The citizens were demoralized. Their fortifications were inadequate and their ammunition nonexistent. Their chief military asset was Old John Brown, who stalked the streets advising everyone not to panic and to fire low. Geary went into conference with the newly released Charles Robinson and other Free Soil leaders. Scouts interrupted them to report that Atchison's army had turned and was moving back to Missouri. Lawrencians were satisfied. So was Geary and he returned to Lecompton with the troops.

There he was puzzled by a communique that read: "In obedience to the call of Acting-Governor Woodson, I have organized a militia force of about eight hundred men, who are now in the field, ready for duty and impatient to act. Hearing of your arrival, I beg leave to report to you for orders." It was signed by one Brigadier General William Heiskill. A quick check revealed that Daniel Woodson had not delivered Geary's proclamations calling for the Proslavery army to disband.

At about the same time, a message came from Lawrence saying that Atchison's retreat had been a ruse. He had wheeled and was marching again on Lawrence.

Back to Lawrence went Geary and his dragoons. The governor spent the night reassuring the Free Soilers. In the morning, the Border Army massed at Franklin and formed for an attack. Geary rode to meet them. He encountered an advance guard of three hundred men. He was challenged, and in turn he counterchallenged. The riders told him they were part of the territorial militia called by his excellency the governor of Kansas and that they "were marching to wipe out Lawrence and every damned abolitionist in the country." Geary identified himself as his excellency the governor of Kansas and demanded to be taken to their officers.

The Border Army had drawn up on a broad plain near the juncture of the Kansas and Wakarusa rivers. Reports of its size had not been exaggerated. It was twenty-seven hundred strong—mounted companies, infantry and a strong battery of six-pound cannons. The old, familiar crew was in command: Ex-Senator Atchison, Stringfellow, Territorial Delegate Whitfield, George Clarke and Titus. Supreme Court Justice Sterling Cato and Sheriff Jones were there too, giving a semblance of legality.

Geary met them strongly. He reaffirmed the position he had taken in his inaugural address and reminded them that, by his two proclamations, this volunteer militia was now an illegal body. If force were the only thing to which Free Soilers would respond, then *he* would employ such force.

General Clarke said he'd fight the cavalry before he'd give up this expedition. But the others, who had no desire to fight federal troops, talked him down.

The Missourians retired from the field with Atchison saying, "He promised us all we wanted."

Free Soilers suspected this might be true, particularly since more than one hundred Free Soilers from Colonel Harvey's command had just been imprisoned at Lecompton.

Analyzing Woodson's three weeks of power and the first few days of Geary's reign, historian L. W. Spring stated flatly that "If Woodson's administration could have been stretched into a few days more of life, the complete conquest of Lawrence and of Kansas would have been assured."

Tired, the new governor headed back to Lecompton.

The Kickapoo Rangers had preceded him, pillaging most of the Free Soil homes along the way. At one cabin the governor's party found a man writhing in the dirt by his gate. He was Free Soiler David C. Buffum and he was dying. The Kickapoo Rangers had spied his horses and set to rounding them up. Buffum, who was lame, begged to keep them—they were all he had, and a large family was dependent upon him. One of the Rangers, a man named Hays, called him a God-damned abolitionist and shot him in the stomach. Then the Rangers led off the horses, leaving Buffum to die.

Back in Lecompton, Geary ordered Hays arrested immediately. Then he went to view the Free Soil prisoners. They were a motley crew penned in a tent compound guarded by federal troops. Under Colonel Harvey this group had attacked the Proslavery town of Hickory Point, which had defied Lane on the general's latest jaunt to Nebraska. The town surrendered after an extended and noisy battle in which only one man, Proslavery, had been killed. Both sides celebrated the end of hostilities by sitting down together and guzzling whiskey. Harvey's men were in no shape to resist when federal troops arrived and took them into custody.

Geary also discovered a jail full of other Free Soil prisoners being held without bail on a variety of dubious charges. He called in Judges Cato and Lecompte and set about trying to reform the judiciary. First on the list were trials for all current prisoners. The governor felt that the arrest of Hays was also of pressing urgency, and since no action had yet been taken he offered a five hundred dollar reward for the man.

After some three weeks delay, Judge Cato got around to Harvey's men—in the true service of justice he committed the entire party to stand trial on the charge of first degree murder. One hundred and one Free Soilers were to be tried for the death of one Proslavery man. Naturally, bail was out of the question.

In the interim, Charles Hays had been arrested. Not by any territorial officer, but by one of Geary's special agents. The evidence against Hays was so overwhelming that even the solidly Proslavery jury had to return an indictment for murder. Justice Lecompte promptly admitted Hays to bail with Sheriff Jones standing bond. Proslavery men enjoyed that one. It was well known that Jones didn't have a dollar to his name. Geary denounced Lecompte's action as "judicial outrage without precedent" and ordered Hays rearrested. When Hays was brought in, Lecompte secured him on a writ of habeas corpus and again released him to Sheriff Jones.

Geary gave up. Although he couldn't keep Hays in jail, he had made an important gain: Free Soilers now believed he would use his fullest power to administer justice impartially.

The judiciary squabble lasted through the fall, but Kansas—to everyone's surprise—began to settle down under Geary's steady and determined hand. Lane was in Nebraska greeting incoming parties of Free Soilers, grandstanding and selling off the horses he had stolen from Proslavery men. Geary had connived to get Old Brown out of the territory; he was traveling East where he would soon be heard roaring from podiums instead of thickets. Two companies of militia—one Proslave under Titus, the other Free Soil under Walker—had been mobilized. Constant federal patrols had edged most of the marauding bands from the field and were successfully dampening outbreaks of potential violence.

Things were looking good in the territory, so good that on November 11 General Smith reported to Washington that "I consider tranquility and order entirely restored in Kansas." Governor Geary designated November 20 as a day of general praise and thanksgiving.

Violence, of course, or its threat, had not simply disappeared; it had only slipped into the background. Its tracks were still clearly visible. Federal troops searched wagons belonging to a party of three hundred men led by Shalor Eldridge and Samuel Pomeroy, found and confiscated "many new saddles and 242 percussion muskets, Hall's muskets, and Sharps carbines, two officers' and 61 common sabres, about 50 Colt revolvers *boxed,* four boxes ball cartridges, &c, &c." They didn't intercept three wagons brought in by nineteen-year-old Preston Plumb. These contained a 12-pound cannon, 250 boxes of Colt revolvers, 250 Bowie knives and 20,000 rounds of ammunition.

But it *looked* like peace. Geary could, for example, point to the resolutions passed by the leaders of Westport, that hotbed of Proslavery sentiment, welcoming all emigrants regardless of their politics. Settlers and money were literally streaming into the territory. Civilization and its amenities were on the march. Anyway, that's how it seemed.

How was Governor Geary to know that the advent of winter always suppressed the more outrageous acts of violence in Kansas? And how was he to know the President's strong support was due mostly to Pierce's desire to make the party look good for the coming election. That same election, in fact, had tamed most of the territory's more volatile elements; nobody wanted to hurt his chances for political success.

The country went to the polls on November 4. The Democrats, Unionism, Slavery and Buchanan carried the day. But an ominous note was sounded. Voting lines were strictly geographic, and Frémont and the infant, more or less abolitionist Republican party, were beaten by less than six hundred thousand votes.

But it was winter in Kansas Territory. And other than the still lively rumors that Lane was going to descend with his Army of the North, there was not much to be concerned about. On the contrary, Governor Geary was brimming with confidence. He wrote to United States Secretary of State William L. Marcy on the last day of 1856 and congratulated the administration and the country on the manner in which Kansas had been tamed. "Crime so rife and daring, at the period of my arrival," he penned, "is almost entirely banished. I can truthfully assure you that, in proportion to her population and extent, less crime is being committed in Kansas than in any other portion of the United States."

Poor, hasty Governor Geary.

The Law and Order party, encouraged by Buchanan's election victory, changed its name to the National Democratic party of Kansas—a one-issue party: slavery. Free Soilers had not been overly disappointed by the elections. The Republicans had made a good showing, Geary was

treating them fairly, and, most importantly, mass emigra-
tion, as Atchison and his cohorts had foreseen, had given
them a population majority.

The idyll ended on January 12, 1857. That was the
day the territorial legislature convened. The Proslavery
party was numerically weaker, but it still had absolute
control of the territory's political machinery. Prior to the
opening of the session, the legislators met and agreed that
any act passed by both sections, but vetoed by Geary,
would automatically be passed over his head. Laws and
lawmaking could wait, though, and the legislators spent
their first few days denouncing and abusing and insulting
the governor in speech after speech. When a message
from him was being read, several expressed their opinion
by jamming their fingers into their ears and refusing to
listen.

When they got down to business, they promptly
awarded territorial judges the right to admit prisoners to
bail whether the offenses had been previously bailable or
not. So much for Geary's attempt to meddle with the
judiciary. The governor just as promptly vetoed the bill
saying it would only increase crimes of the types he had
been trying to stop. Zip, bang! The legislature passed it
over his veto in less than five minutes.

The legislature now drafted a message demanding that
Geary explain why he had not commissioned William
Sherrard to succeed Sam Jones as sheriff of Douglas
County. When Jones had resigned, the county Board of
Supervisors appointed Sherrard to take his place. Sherrard
was a young man, well born and hot-tempered and fond
of alcohol. At first Geary did not issue the commission
simply because it wasn't his job; it was the duty of the

secretary of state, who was absent at the moment. But when Sherrard began visiting the executive offices and shouting and threatening him, the governor grew apprehensive, began to doubt the wisdom of the board's choice. He wasn't alone; the board itself reconsidered and announced it would revoke the appointment.

The House, rabidly Proslave, made the appointment on its own authority. But the Council refused to concur and nothing came of it. Thus the demand for an explanation from Geary.

The governor answered them with a tactful, well reasoned and respectful message. One member of the legislature said the governor should be "strung, quartered, and burned, body and soul." The governor was called a despot and tyrant whose atrocities were more abominable than those of Nero and Caligula.

Geary's continued refusal threw Sherrard into a rage. He went to the legislature the next day, where Geary was attending the session. When Geary rose to leave Sherrard cocked two pistols and aimed them at the governor's back. Geary walked calmly from the building. Sherrard followed him down the street and most likely would have fired if the governor had so much as looked back.

This was too much even for many professional Geary-haters. The Council passed a resolution of condemnation against Sherrard. The House, though, refused to add its own censure.

A mass meeting was called to discuss the problem. In Capital Hall Free Soilers and Proslavery men were jammed together and everyone voiced his opinions while a committee appointed by Proslavery Mayor Stewart met in conference. The committee drew up a resolution approving Geary's impartial and energetic administration and pledged to support him.

When the report was read Sherrard leaped up and shouted, "Any man who will dare to endorse these resolutions is a liar, a scoundrel, and a coward!"

A man named Sheppard endorsed them.

Sherrard whipped out a revolver and fired all six shots. Sheppard was hit three times, but didn't fall. He drew his own pistol. It failed to fire, so he advanced on Sherrard and clubbed him. Sherrard clubbed back. They went at each other until pulled apart.

Scattered shots were sounding across the hall. Sherrard now drew his second pistol and took aim at one of Geary's aides, John A. W. Jones. Jones spotted him and fired first. Sherrard was knocked sprawling with a bullet in his head.

Proslavery men offered five hundred dollars to anyone who would kill John Jones. Jones surrendered to Justice Cato, was indicted for murder, released on five thousand dollars bail when pressure was brought on Cato, then fled the territory.

Proslavery men who had supported Geary in the Sherrard question now returned to ranks, and the legislature sent the governor a new bill. An election to select delegates for a constitutional convention was scheduled for June, which necessitated a census to determine eligible voters. The legislature's bill dictated that all the census takers and all the election judges were to be Proslavery men. Geary said he would approve the bill only if a referendum were included, so that each citizen of the territory could approve or disapprove the constitution once it was drawn up.

He was told frankly that this was impossible because it "would defeat the object of the act, which was to secure, beyond any possibility of doubt, the Territory of Kansas to the South as a slave state."

Geary vetoed the bill. Zip, bang! Passed over his veto.

The governor was beginning to weary of all this. Within the growing tension at Lecompton, he sensed a real threat of violence. He requested two additional companies of troops to supplement the federal force already garrisoned there. He discovered, not entirely to his surprise, that his authorization to call out federal troops had been rescinded. This confirmed what Geary had been suspecting—the administration in Washington had abandoned him.

"My only consolation now," Geary wrote Amos Lawrence on February 25, "is that my labors are properly appreciated by, and that I have the sympathy of, very many of the best citizens of the Union. . . . How much longer I shall be required to sacrifice pecuniary interests, comfort, and health in what appears almost a thankless work remains to be determined."

It was determined in March. On the tenth day, Sam Walker answered a knock late at night and saw Governor Geary, harried looking, with a pistol strapped to either hip.

"I'm going to Washington and I'll straighten things out," he said.

But in Washington, Geary discovered that the new administration was not interested in straightening things out. Nothing was left for him but to resign, which he did, six months from the day he had arrived in Kansas Territory.

9.

FREE SOILERS TAKE OVER

President James Buchanan was an older, more experienced man than Franklin Pierce. The Democratic party placed high hopes in him.

Buchanan took office on March 4, 1857. Two days later Chief Justice Roger Taney of the Supreme Court handed down one of the most significant and charged decisions of the age. The Court had ruled 7 to 2 against a slave named Dred Scott who had petitioned for freedom on the grounds that he had lived several years with his master in free territory and free states. The Court ruled that slaves were property not state by state, but nationally, and that Congress had no constitutional power to bar slavery from the territories. This of course implied that the main goal of Free Soilers and Republicans and even the doctrine of popular sovereignty itself were unconstitutional; for if Congress could not prohibit slavery in the territories, then certainly it could not delegate such power to territorial settlers.

The South, naturally, was greatly cheered. The North

was appalled. Several New England abolitionist societies swore they would defy the law at every opportunity, and the consequences be damned.

In Kansas, the Court's ruling was interpreted as a validation of the Proslavery legislature's enactments.

Kansas was again without a governor and this time there was not even a secretary of state to fill the post. Shortly after Geary left, Daniel Woodson was given the more desirable post of Receiver of the Delaware Lands. It was not until mid-April that an administrator appeared —Frederick P. Stanton, the territory's new secretary of state. Stanton came in warily, with caution. Kansas, he knew, was a wild beast, and he was determined not to provoke it. So all he did was apportion delegates to the constitutional convention.

Frederick P. Stanton had seized the beast's tail and given it a sharp twist.

He had, innocently enough, based the apportionment on the recent census, the one designed by the Proslavery legislature to be deliberately defective. Free Soilers had not registered. They were sure that federal territorial officials would not dare call an election on the basis of a fraudulent census. But, as was usual when Free Soilers boycotted political procedure, their strategy only put them in worse shape.

The new governor, Robert J. Walker, arrived in the territory on May 27, 1857. Walker was a tough, shrewd little intellectual, a financial wizard and an excellent politician with an impressive list of accomplishments behind him.

His inaugural address was a firm statement of a policy

that intended to hew hard and close to the middle of the road. If the present legislature was invalid, he pointed out, then all legal and judicial transactions in the territory to date were also invalid, all land titles were void and Kansas was completely without law. Therefore the legislature must be supported. He raked Free Soilers for their intended abstention from the constitutional delegate election, and he gave his word that no man's right to vote would be contravened and that nonresidents of Kansas would be prevented from casting ballots. He further promised that any constitution framed would be submitted to the people for acceptance or rejection. Of slavery itself, he suggested that the climate of Kansas might not be suited to that institution. But, he said, even if there were no slavery in Kansas he trusted that it would not become a state controlled by the treasonous fanaticism of abolitionism. He also detailed programs through which Kansas, on gaining statehood, would be completely free of debt.

Kansans couldn't have cared less about state debts and taxes at the moment. Slavery was their issue, and slavery was what they wanted to hear about.

It would seem that Walker's statements would have been, if not pleasing, at least satisfactory to both sides.

But this was a contest of extremes, not compromise, and both Free Soilers and Proslavery men believed the new governor to be cuddling up too much to the opposition. Therefore, everyone considered him an enemy.

But Walker was secure in the knowledge that Washington stood solidly behind him. He had accepted the governorship only after President Buchanan and Stephen

Douglas, then Senate majority leader, had promised him that the people of the territory would indeed be allowed to determine their own institutions, and determine them unmolested.

Actually, Buchanan and his advisers had in mind something a little different. It was obvious that the South would be appeased by nothing less than absolute control of Kansas. The administration had expected the little governor discreetly to follow the party line, and Buchanan and his cabinet were not pleased by Walker's inaugural statements. But sudden recall and replacement were considered too risky.

Three important events were on the territorial slate: (1) the election of constitutional delegates in June, (2) the election of legislators in October, and (3) the convention to frame the constitution in November.

Walker urged Free Soilers to get out and vote. If they wished to change things, he said, then they were only acting like spoiled, petulant, self-defeating children by staying away from the polls. The new governor talked up a storm, Free Soilers agreed, but then *he* had never been chased from polls with gunfire and had never witnessed invasion by a Missouri voting army.

Because of the imbalanced apportionment the outcome of the June election was a foregone conclusion. The only real question was which of the available Proslavery delegates would be selected. But the October elections, now that might be another matter—if the governor meant what he said.

Free Soilers began gathering in Topeka for the convening of their illegal and interdicted legislature. Governor Walker was there to address them. Should they attempt to enact and enforce a code of laws, he said, there could be only one result—"absolute, clear, direct and positive collision between that legislature and the government of the United States." He again promised unconditionally that any constitution framed would be submitted to *all* the people for a full and honest vote. Free Soilers listened, then opened their session and staged a show that was entirely for his benefit. Hours of hot rhetoric went by, all designed to convince the governor of one thing—if Free Soilers weren't treated fairly there would be a massive and bloody rebellion.

Walker was convinced. He wrote to Washington and said that had it not been for his presence and his pledges, the territory would have plunged into general civil war then and there.

The election of delegates took place on June 15 with hardly a snarl from the Kansas beast. Missourians, like Free Soilers, stayed home, and only a small percentage of the Proslavery men in the territory bothered to cast ballots. One candidate received a single vote—but that was enough to elect him. The election, naturally, was a clean sweep for the Proslavery party; nobody else ran.

A short time later Leavenworth, that former stronghold of southern radicalism, elected a Free Soil mayor and at the expense of only one life. A young Georgian pulled a knife on a Free Soil German and was promptly stabbed to death in return. Money had made the difference. Emigrants were arriving by the thousands, bringing money, and the prospect of quick fortunes tended to erode, or at least restrain, ideological differences rather quickly. Leavenworth was booming and Free Soilers, who had once feared to walk its streets, were now the majority.

Kansas passed its summer uneasily, but in comparative peace. Businessmen and merchants who had settled early found their capital increasing at a surprisingly pleasant rate. Prosperity was beginning to hobble the influence of extremists.

But peace was still a long, long way off. Lawrence, for example, refused to organize under the charter granted by the territorial legislature. Instead, it set up an independent government. Walker considered this an act of rebellion. He wrote to Washington: "Lawrence is the hotbed of all abolition movements in the Territory. It is filled with a considerable number of mercenaries, who are paid by the Abolition Societies to perpetuate and diffuse agitation throughout Kansas, and prevent a peaceful settlement of the question." He then called out the cavalry, which marched on Lawrence three hundred strong. It was all rather embarrassing, though, for no overt crime had been committed and no one seemed the least bit interested in the soldiers. So the troops withdrew, having accomplished nothing, not even sure why they had gone there in the first place.

Affluence added a new twist to Kansas violence—the first murder for money was committed late in July. Now this was really too much to bear. Killing a man for his beliefs was an honorable thing, but killing a man for his money apparently shocked Kansans to the roots of their sensibilities. Two thousand Free Soilers and Pro-slavery men set aside their personal grievances long enough to form a mob, storm the Leavenworth jail, drag out the two murderers and lynch them.

Justice having been satisfied, the resident Kansans returned to the business at hand. The Proslavery party nominated its legislative candidates. Free Soilers held a passionate series of meetings trying to decide whether or not they were going to vote. Moderates were eager to meet the Southerners at the polls. Extremists were violently opposed, condemning participation as a back-down of principle. Ominously, Free Soil leaders authorized Lane to put the Free Soil militia on a war footing.

The squabbling peaked at the large Grasshopper Falls convention in late August. Robinson's moderates carried the day. Although committed to vote, the Free Soilers were not optimistic. A committee report cited the instances of disfranchised voters, the probability of another invasion by Missouri voters, Proslavery election judges and, perhaps most important, the question of whether or not Governor Walker would live up to his word.

They need not have worried about Walker. He sent federal troops into nearly half the voting districts with strict orders to prevent all illegal voting and to safeguard the rights of all qualified voters. Under the shadow of federal arms, the election was the most nonviolent in the territory's history. Even Kickapoo could come up with nothing more than a nonfatal, half-hearted brawl.

When the election returns were in, Governor Walker knew immediately that his troop contingents had been short by two. McGee County was a Cherokee Indian Reservation with only a handful of resident whites.

Three months earlier, in the constitutional delegate election, 14 votes had been cast there. Now McGee County turned in 1226 votes. The town of Oxford, in Johnson County, was a mudhole of six houses. Yet Oxford proudly reported 1628 votes.

Obviously all was not right in McGee County and in Oxford.

Here was a Class-A Kansas Territory problem for Governor Walker. With the two fraudulent returns, the territorial legislature would remain in Proslavery hands. Without them, Free Soilers would take over.

Walker *was* a man of his word. He had promised honest elections, and honest they would be. He dumped the Oxford and McGee votes. The final score: Free Soilers 9 of the 13 councilmen's seats and 24 of the 39 representatives' seats.

Free Soilers were jubilant, Proslavery men furious. Justice Sterling Cato issued a mandamus—a binding court order—instructing the governor to certify the excluded Proslavery candidates. Walker ignored the mandamus. Ex-Sheriff Jones was one of those unseated candidates. He stormed into Secretary Frederick P. Stanton's office and demanded his certification. Stanton was intimidated neither by Jones nor by Jones's gun and ordered him out. A party of Free Soilers visited Stanton the next day and offered to string Jones up before dawn. Stanton politely declined.

Governor Walker was enraged by the actions of Jones and other Proslavery men. He slipped a multibarreled pepperbox pistol into his pocket, took Stanton by the arm and marched off to the nearest saloon. He spent the evening visiting the various saloons and meeting places of Proslavery men in Lecompton and told them in very plain English precisely what he thought of them and what they could do with themselves.

The Proslavery party knew it was in trouble, but it still held an ace—the constitutional convention. The delegates met in Lecompton in October. Hundreds of Free Soilers flocked there too, apparently for no other purpose than to frolic and to taunt the Proslavery delegates.

The constitution drafted bore great resemblance to state constitutions that had been successful in the past, and was essentially a good one. It differed radically, however, from previous documents on the issue of slavery. "The right of property," it read, "is before and higher than any constitutional sanction, and the right of the owner of a slave to such slave and its increase is the same and as inviolable as the right of any property whatever."

How, though, did one go about saddling such a tenet on a population that was overwhelming antislave?

The answer lay in a *qualified* submission to the voters. Only the slavery article would go before the people. They could vote for "Constitution with slavery" or "Constitution with no slavery." The delegates tacked a kicker on the latter choice. If the territory chose constitution without slavery, then the article would read: "Slavery shall no longer exist in the State of Kansas, except that the right of property in slaves now in this territory shall in no manner be interfered with." This meant, of course, that the children of slaves now in the territory would be slaves, and that the children of those children would be slaves, and that . . .

Free Soilers compared the choice to the old witchcraft test in which the accused was bound and thrown into water. If she sank and drowned, she was considered not guilty. If she floated, she was judged guilty, taken out and burned. If they voted for constitution without slavery, then they themselves would guarantee the right of slavery in Kansas so long as slaves bore issue.

Various Proslavery men also objected. They claimed that the "Black Republicans" would make mountains of political hay from this tactic. Others suggested that it had been the inspiration of Free State Democrats who desired a federal backlash to toss the rigged referendum out. But the majority supported the device. The referendum was to take place on December 21. Two weeks later, on January 4, the territory would elect officers under its new constitution.

Free Soilers held a series of protest meetings. The largest met in early December and was presided over by Charles Robinson. It passed a resolution which read:

> Appealing to the God of Justice and Humanity, we do solemnly enter into league and covenant with each other that we will never, under any circumstances, permit the said constitution, so framed and not submitted, to be the organic law for the State of Kansas, but do pledge our lives, our fortunes, and our sacred honor in ceaseless hostility to the same.

Governor Walker could do nothing. He had been outfoxed by the Proslavery party, and abandoned by the administration in Washington. He went back East, as his predecessor had done, to straighten things out. Like Geary, he never returned.

When President Buchanan opened the Thirty-fifth Congress of the United States on December 7, 1857, he endorsed the Proslave Lecompton Constitution. He said, "The Kansas-Nebraska Bill did not require the submission of any portion of the Constitution to an election, except that which relates to the domestic institution of slavery." And therefore he urged Congress to grant statehood to Kansas under that document.

On that same day in Kansas the territorial legislature met in special session, called by Acting-Governor Stanton under Free Soil pressure. Stanton had resisted, pointing out that officially the terms of the newly elected Free Soilers had not yet begun. Stanton knew full well that such a session would be his political death warrant. But Free Soilers left him no choice. The session was called—and Washington removed Stanton from office nine days later.

Free Soilers boiled into Lecompton by the hundreds. When enough lawmakers could be dragged from celebrations to make a quorum, the legislature denounced the Lecompton Constitution and named January 4 as the day on which the entire document would be submitted to the people. A third choice would be added to the existing two—"Against the constitution framed at Lecompton." Then, disregarding Stanton's veto, the legislators made the Free State Militia the official territorial militia and placed James H. Lane in command.

On December 21 Free Soilers boycotted the slavery

referendum. With none but Proslavery men voting, constitution with slavery was passed by a nearly unanimous 6226 votes—approximately half cast by border-crossing Missourians.

On that day Kansas Territory also received a new acting-governor, General John W. Denver. Denver was a Virginian, a respected lawyer and veteran of the Mexican War, currently holding the office of Indian Commissioner. He had been reluctant to accept the Kansas post on the grounds that he was a personal friend of ex-Senator Atchison and other leading Missourians and he did not want to tempt them to ask him to perform his duties in a biased way.

The question now before Free Soilers was: Should they nominate candidates for offices under the Lecompton constitution on the possibility that Kansas might be admitted to the Union with that document? A mass meeting was held in Lawrence. Charles Robinson and the moderates said yes, citing the good results of their participation in the legislative election. The radicals, as usual, wanted nothing to do with it. The question was being put to a vote when a prominent Free Soiler rushed into the room crying "War has begun!" He told the assembly that James Lane and two hundred men were under attack by a huge Proslavery force near Mound City.

While Sam Wood called for volunteers to relieve Lane, the vote was hastily concluded. Tempers were raging and a Free Soil slate was ruled out—precisely what Lane had wanted.

A day and a half later, Lane was back in Lawrence,

looking well rested and content. And properly so, inasmuch as the battle had been nothing but the product of his imagination. But conservative and moderate Free Soilers had gone ahead and nominated a ticket anyway, so the Grim Chieftain, after brief reflection, joined them on the bandwagon. He was one of the firmest territorial believers in the maxim, "If you can't lick 'em, join 'em." To the old saw Lane seemed to add *and fast.*

Free Soilers then went to the polls and rejected the Lecompton Constitution overwhelmingly.

A Missouri voting army attacked again in the election of constitutional officers, contributing more than a third of the Proslave vote, but Free Soilers held the edge despite them. When a federal committee arrived to investigate the votes, John C. Calhoun, chairman of the Lecompton Constitutional Convention and custodian of the election returns, abruptly left the territory. His chief clerk, Lauchlan A. MacLean, told the committee regretfully that they could not investigate the returns— he had forwarded them to Calhoun.

But Sam Walker, who was now sheriff, learned from an informer that the returns were hidden in MacLean's woodpile. Armed with a search warrant he recovered them. The findings of the federal committee were a painful embarrassment to Proslavery partisans.

The Southerners were growing demoralized. Titus went off to South America on a freebooting expedition. Firebrand John Stringfellow put his *Squatter Sovereign* up for sale and returned to Missouri. Others smelled a lost cause in the wind and left the territory. The slavery question in Kansas, wrote Stringfellow, had been settled against the South by immigration.

The struggle, however, was not yet over.

Denver wrote to President Buchanan detailing the state of affairs and urgently advising the Chief Executive to disregard the Lecompton Constitution and allow Kansans to make a fresh start. But Buchanan yielded to southern pressure, abandoned his earlier pledge to Walker, and sent the Lecompton Constitution to Congress on February 2, 1858, with a special message in which he requested that Kansas be speedily admitted to the Union.

The South was divided. Several politicians felt that to admit Kansas would be for all practical purposes to hand the North another state. Debate over the territory once again filled Congress. Senator James H. Hammond of South Carolina called the history of the Kansas Territory a disgusting one from beginning to end. North Carolina's Senator Biggs doubted whether Kansans were of sufficient character for enlightened self-government. Representative Thomas L. Anderson of Missouri called the settlers ungovernable, reckless people. Senator Alfred Iverson of Georgia said: "Why, sir, if you could rake the infernal regions from the center to the circumference and from the surface to the bottom, you could not fish up such a mass of infamous corruption as exists in some portions of Kansas."

The argumentation filled more than nine hundred pages of the *Congressional Globe.* Stephen A. Douglas had the fortitude to stand behind the doctrine he had promulgated. He described the Proslavery refusal to submit the entire constitution as treacherous and insisted that the doctrine of popular sovereignty demanded a referendum of the complete document.

But Senator Trusten Polk of Missouri, defending the Lecompton Constitution, saw the territory's history as a "majestic spectacle of the people marching in stately pace to the accomplishment of their purposes." He articulated the most effective argument in favor of the Lecompton Constitution: it was the work of a legitimate convention that had observed all the necessary formalities.

On March 23 the Senate voted to admit Kansas under the Lecompton Constitution. The House voted against admission and passed another bill that would refer the constitution back to the people for ratification. The Senate would not approve this. A committee from both chambers was formed to effect a compromise.

The English Bill resulted. The territory had requested a land grant of twenty-three million acres. The English Bill reduced this to a little less than four million. If Kansans rejected the greatly diminished grant, then they automatically rejected the Lecompton Constitution and would continue as a territory until a population of ninety-four thousand was reached. Acceptance would mean acceptance of the constitution and statehood.

The committee's majority report insisted this was not a device through which to submit the document to a popular referendum, but that is precisely what it was.

Kansas rendered its decision on August 2. With 13,088 votes cast, it turned down the Lecompton Constitution 7 to 1.

10.

JAYHAWKING

The major events in the history of Kansas Territory occurred within a radius of thirty miles from Lawrence. But several of the most violent confrontations and much of the more blatant lawlessness took place in the southeastern regions. This was more primitive land than the north, less populated, cut off from the important river transportation and dominated in the early period by the Proslavery party. Its principal town was Fort Scott, a military post abandoned by the government in 1854. By 1856 it was a Border Ruffian stronghold.

There wasn't much for the southeastern Proslavery men to do in the first two years after the signing of the Kansas-Nebraska Act, but when Reid and his men moved against Osawatomie after Old Brown's Pottawatomie Massacre in 1856, one hundred fifty Proslavery men gathered at Fort Scott and marched north to help. As they settled into camp ten miles below Osawatomie they were surprised by a shouting and firing force of Free Soil guerrillas one hundred strong. The Southerners took to their

heels, evidently of lesser stuff than their Missouri com-
patriots, abandoned their black flag inscribed "Victory or
Death," and did not stop until they reached Fort Scott.
They roused the town, shouting in panic that a Free Soil
army was about to put Fort Scott to torch and sword.
Men, women and children evacuated the old fort—and
crept back with shamed faces the next morning when the
Free Soilers failed to materialize.

A few months later ex-Indian Agent George Clarke led
a force of Missourians into those portions of the southeastern territory where Free Soilers had lately begun to
settle. The Border Raiders wreaked general havoc, tearing
down fences, driving off livestock, looting and burning
homes. An old man who later testified before an investigating commission said: "I was in the Black Hawk war,
and have fought in the wars of the United States, and
have received two land-warrants from Washington City
for my services, but I never saw anything so bad and
mean in my life as I saw under General Clarke."

Southeastern Free Soilers had nearly no organization
before Clarke's raid. But now they banded together under
the leadership of James Montgomery. Montgomery was a
bold, cunning, black-bearded ex-preacher of medium
height who had been among the first Free Soilers to settle
southeastern Kansas. Montgomery crossed into Missouri
masquerading as a teacher, got a job and held it for two
weeks while he compiled a list of the men who had been
with Clarke. Then he left, picked up a troop of Free
Soilers, returned, captured twenty of the raiders and
stripped them of their weapons, horses and all valuables.

Encouraged by this success, Montgomery and his men
took the offensive. In the following months they drove

scores of Proslavery families from the territory. Threats were usually sufficient. If not, then robbery did the trick, or home burning, or, if necessary, a near fatal beating. What had begun as an organization of self-defense quickly deteriorated into a band of brigands who much preferred looting to working. Proslavery attempts to resist were brushed aside with relative ease.

Montgomery's men brought the word Jayhawkers into common parlance; the jayhawk was a predatory bird native to Ireland that worried and toyed with its prey. They sent accounts to Lawrence and to correspondents of national newspapers describing outrages committed by raiding Missourians. These were mostly apocryphal, designed to justify their own depredations and build a reputation for themselves as patriots struggling against great odds.

But Proslavery resistance stiffened toward the end of 1857, reinvigorated by the Dred Scott decision and the position of Buchanan's administration. The Jayhawkers sent a delegation to Lane in late December and asked for help. Ordinarily Lane would have gone galloping back with the emissaries, but he was busy trying to persuade Free Soilers to boycott the January 4 elections.

In his place he sent Captain J. B. Abbott and a small company of men. They arrived in time to sit in at one of the Jayhawkers' kangaroo land courts, which was being held in a cabin yard. Abbott was honored by being named judge. Typically, a Free Soiler had charged a Proslavery man with claim jumping. The Northerners had long since given up Federal Judge Williams's court at Fort Scott; he never once ruled in favor of a Free Soil man.

News of this trial—complete with titular jury, counsel

for the complainant and counsel for the defense—reached
United States Marshal Blake Little in Fort Scott. Little immediately deputized a posse and rode to the site of the
trial. The court was warned of Little's approach and it set
aside the land dispute and prepared to fight. Little entered
the scene peacefully, though, and politely requested Montgomery to explain this illegal proceeding. Montgomery
gravely informed the marshal that the legislature had
just repealed the original territorial code enacted at
Shawnee Mission. Thus, until a new code could be framed,
there were no laws for Little to enforce.

The marshal accepted this fantasy and rode back to
Fort Scott. He was nearly laughed out of town. He
deputized a posse of forty men and went thundering back,
afire with indignation and the need for vengeance. He deployed his men in the woods, then approached the open-
air court.

"Gentlemen," he said, "you will understand that you
are dealing with the United States, and not with border
ruffians. You will learn that there is a difference between
them. I order you to surrender and prepare to accompany
me to Fort Scott." He gave the Free Soilers half an hour.
"You will come with me, then, or I'll blow you all to
hell."

He returned to his posse, waited, went back and found
that the Free Soilers had taken cover in and around the
cabin. The marshal ordered a charge. His posse began
bravely enough, but broke completely when a dozen
Sharps rifles barked out. Little's deputies were mostly
loafers and rowdies who had come along for the fun of
things. They had no desire to get shot, so after a couple

of wild answering rounds, they wheeled their mounts and spurred their way back to Fort Scott.

The trial resumed. The Proslavery man was found guilty and ordered out of the territory.

While the southeastern counties were conducting their private, local version of the war for Kansas, and while Congress was wrangling over the Lecompton Constitution in Washington, the territorial legislature opened its session in Lecompton in January 1858. The Topeka Free Soil Legislature was on hand too, meeting jointly with the legitimate territorial organization, amiably requesting that body to vote itself out of existence and transfer all rights and prerogatives to the Topeka Legislature. The argument advanced by Free Soil "Governor" Charles Robinson and his faction was that no matter how the territorial legislature had been purged and revolutionized, it would always bear the stench of its origin.

The newly elected legislators wisely declined this action. It would be suicide for the Free Soil cause, they pointed out, to abolish the legal body and replace it with a substitute that had been ruled treasonous by the federal government. Such a move might well cause the deliberating Congress to accept Kansas into the Union under the odious Lecompton Constitution. This stand rang the death knell for the extralegal and now obsolete Free Soil legislature.

Those who had expected a dramatic change in the Free Soil-controlled legislature were disappointed. Its first session was spent mainly incorporating cities and towns and granting business charters. The single important piece of legislation was the repeal of the laws punishing of-

fenses against slave property. Acting-Governor Denver
used his veto, saying that although the existing laws were
harsh, there had to be some sort of law on the subject so
long as slaves existed in the territory. True to Kansas
tradition, the legislature passed the repeal over his veto.

Next the new legislators tried to move the capital from
Lecompton to an empty stretch of prairie they called
Minneola. Thirty-five of their fifty-two-man total had
financial interests in this move. Denver vetoed the bill.
The legislators overruled his veto with a speed equal to
that of their Proslavery predecessors. But Denver was not
to be beaten. He simply refused to move from Lecompton
and would not allow the records and governmental documents to be transferred. He was backed by the United
States Attorney General who ruled the scheme unconstitutional. So the planned site of Minneola remained grass,
brush and weeds.

Legislative sessions were limited by law to forty days.
Three days before adjournment, the lawmakers passed a
bill authorizing a new constitutional convention. Denver
decided the territory had had more than its share of con-
stitution-making for the present, so he took advantage of
a law that granted him absolute veto power over any
bill reaching his desk within three days of a session's end,
a pocket veto.

But the legislators were not so easily put off. Just prior
to adjournment, they sent him a document that purported
to be the bill, which they alleged to have passed over his
veto. It was an outright forgery—Denver still had the
original in his hands. He summoned the speaker of the
house, the president of the council and the chief clerk,

confronted them with the evidence and demanded to know whose idea it was.

Jim Lane's.

Denver's response to that answer is not recorded. What is recorded though, is that he gave them a choice: sign a statement saying the original bill had never been returned to them and had not been passed over his veto, or destroy the forgery in his presence. They opted for the latter.

The legislators, however, were of hardy stuff and in the closing hours of the session they voted unanimously that the bill had indeed been duly passed. They scheduled both the election of delegates and the constitutional convention for March.

The election was held and the delegates assembled at the almost nonexistent town of Minneola two weeks later. Immediately, violent debate raged over the convention site and a motion was passed to move to Leavenworth. Relocated, the delegates got down to work and produced a very good state constitution.

As the details of the new constitution were being hammered out, two Free Soilers were being murdered in the Fort Scott vicinity. In answer, Montgomery's Jayhawkers took to their saddles and went on a pillaging and burning spree.

Acting-Governor Denver sent Captain Weaver and a company of federal dragoons downstate to restore order. An officer and thirty soldiers overtook Montgomery and seven of his men not far from Fort Scott. They gave chase. The Jayhawkers retreated to a ravine, dismounted and unlimbered their Sharps rifles. Sabers in hand, the dragoons charged. Montgomery called for them to halt.

The troops had no intention of taking orders from a Jay-hawker.

Montgomery and his men volleyed their rifles, then opened up with revolvers. The officer and one enlisted man fell dead from their saddles, four more dropped wounded. The rest of the squadron drew back, and Montgomery and his men escaped.

It was a boost to local Free Soilers' morale, wrote one of Montgomery's contemporaries, to have it "satisfactorily demonstrated that a Sharps rifle ball, carefully directed, would have the same effect upon a dragoon as on a common man."

One of the more important Proslavery men in south-eastern Kansas was Charles A. Hamilton. Hamilton was a handsome, wealthy young Georgian whose father had contributed one thousand dollars to the Southern Emigrant Aid Company. The Hamilton family was not noted for its pacifism and prior to emigrating to Kansas Territory in 1856, Charles had been wounded in a feud. Hamilton grew progressively angrier as he watched the Proslavery faction cower in the face of Montgomery's Jay-hawkers. Finally, he drew up a list of local Free Soilers he considered particularly repellent. He planned to capture and execute them.

But the death list somehow fell into Montgomery's hands and following his fight with the dragoons, the Jayhawker led an attack against Hamilton's large and fortified house. Captain Weaver had taken the rest of his troops to the field when the ravaged patrol came limping back to Fort Scott. He located and attacked Montgomery in the middle of the assault on Hamilton's house, drove him off, but failed to capture him.

The two confrontations with federal troops and the abortive attempt on Hamilton's house dampened the spirits of both sides and the next six weeks passed in relative calm. On May 12, Acting-Governor Denver became Governor Denver. On May 18, the Leavenworth Constitution was submitted to a referendum. It was a poor showing, only four thousand ballots cast. Kansans were as disgusted with the "Minneola Swindle" as they had been with the "Lecompton Swindle," and they turned down this excellent constitution because of the stigma of its origin.

One day after the Leavenworth Constitution was defeated Charles Hamilton and some forty proslavery men staged the southern rendition of Old Brown's Pottawattomie Massacre. They appeared in the morning at Trading Post, a small settlement on the border, south of Kansas City, broke into groups and set about rounding up Free Soilers. They met several hours later, shepherding a sizeable number of prisoners. Hamilton selected eleven and set the rest free. The Proslavery men marched their victims to a nearby gulch on the Marais des Cygnes and lined them up against the embankment.

"Gentlemen," one of the Free Soilers said, "if you are going to shoot, take good aim."

Hamilton ordered his men to draw their weapons. A Border Ruffian wheeled his horse out of line and told Hamilton he wouldn't participate in "any such goddamned piece of business as this." Hamilton shrugged, cocked his pistol aimed at the Free Soilers and fired. A general volley followed—and the eleven Free Soilers crumpled to the ground.

Five were dead, five were wounded and one was unharmed. Those who still lived feigned death. The Proslavery men hastily turned out the Free Soilers' pockets, taking everything of value. One of the wounded men groaned. A pistol was leveled at his head and discharged. The bullet went through the man's cheeks, nearly severed the base of his tongue, but did not kill him.

Poet John Greenleaf Whittier immortalized the massacre in a poem that appeared in the *Atlantic Monthly* four months later. It began:

> A blush as of roses,
> 　Where roses never grew!
> Great drops on the bunch grass,
> 　But not of the dew!

Montgomery's reaction to the slaughter was to go on a jayhawking spree, raiding almost as far north as the town of Lecompton. Apparently, Denver did not lay responsibility wholly, or even chiefly, on the heads of Proslavery men. He dispatched Sam Walker, who had risen from the office of sheriff to deputy marshal, to the Fort Scott area with a warrant for Montgomery's arrest.

At Raysville, fifteen miles north of Fort Scott, Walker found a large gathering of Free Soilers. Montgomery was calling for the destruction of Fort Scott. Walker, ardent Free Soiler that he was, had no desire to arrest the Jayhawker. He remained in the background until someone recognized him and asked what he was doing there. He'd been sent to arrest Montgomery, he answered, but he claimed he didn't know the man by sight and that he did not wish to have him pointed out.

Montgomery launched into a passionate denunciation of the territory's officials. They sent down agents to arrest Free Soil men, he said, but they ignored Fort Scott, which even at this very moment was sheltering some of the men who had committed the Marais des Cygnes Massacre. Walker rose and identified himself to the assembly. If someone would get him the warrants, he said, then he would make arrests in Fort Scott.

There was no one available to issue proper warrants, so Sam Walker asked for a common justice's writ even though he admitted that as a federal officer he could not legally serve it. The deputy marshal entered Fort Scott on May 30. Montgomery—who was still incognito by tacit understanding—and a volunteer posse of Free Soilers rode with him. They went directly to the house of General George Clarke. Proslavery guns were aimed point blank at them. The posse in turn aimed point blank at Clarke, who stood in his doorway undecided as to whether or not he would surrender.

Finally, ashen-faced, he did. Walker and the Free Soilers took several other prisoners and left without a shot having been fired. Surprisingly, Walker then placed Montgomery under arrest.

Nobody has ever explained what happened next, but all Walker's prisoners escaped, and the deputy marshal arrived back in Lecompton empty-handed.

On June 3, General James H. Lane shot Free Soiler Gaius Jenkins to death in Lawrence and was almost lynched. Jenkins and Lane had quarreled violently for some months over a land claim. Free Soilers' loyalties were divided: New Englanders backed Jenkins, Midwesterners, Lane. Lane's cabin stood on the disputed land. On the morning of the killing, Jenkins, carrying a rifle, went with an armed party of friends to Lane's cabin. Jenkins set aside his rifle, took up an axe and broke down a section of Lane's fence. Lane stood in the yard with a shotgun and warned Jenkins and his party not to enter. Earlier in the day Jenkins had told Sheriff Sam Walker that he was going to Lane's and that he was going to have either "water or blood." Jenkins and his men passed through the broken fence. Much contradictory evidence was given in court concerning what happened next. Some witnesses claim that a member of Jenkins' party fired at Lane with a pistol. Others said Jenkins attacked Lane with the axe. And still others maintained that the Grim Chieftain, without any aggressive move having been made against him, blasted Jenkins down in cold blood. Whatever the case, several qiuck shots were fired (only one from Lane's single-barreled shotgun), and when it was over, Jenkins lay dead and Lane had been wounded in the knee.

A crowd gathered, the bulk of it friends of Jenkins. Ex-Sheriff Jones was present too and for once in his life he was not fussy about the company he kept. He joined the New England Free Soilers wholeheartedly, yelling "Lynch him! Lynch him!" at the top of his lungs.

Mob action was prevented by Sam Walker who walked up to Lane, put him into custody and drove him off to jail. A grand jury found no grounds for an indictment and Lane was released. The killing damaged his reputation—but only for a while. Before long Lane, in his inimitable style, was turning it into an advantage. In the middle of speeches he would shout:

> They say Jim Lane is a murderer, yes a murderer! What are the facts? When the noble women of Lawrence were endeavoring to establish a public library, what did Jim Lane do? He took his old claybank horse out of the field where he was plowing to raise a little corn for his family, and sold that horse for $37.50 and gave the money to those noble women and yet, great God, they say Jim Lane is a murderer.

His listeners were thrilled. No one stopped to wonder just what kind of explanatory relationship there was between selling an old claybank horse and killing Gaius Jenkins.

The affair with Walker at Fort Scott had left the Jayhawkers unsatisfied, so on June 6 Montgomery swept down on the town in the middle of the night, silenced the sentries, put a few buildings to the torch and then retired to a nearby ravine. An alarm was raised and shortly Fort Scott's residents were rushing to put out the flames. The Jayhawkers opened fire. Several Proslavery men were wounded; the rest dispersed hurriedly, grabbed weapons and took cover. Shots were exchanged for a short time, then the Free Soilers withdrew.

Governor Denver scented an explosion in the wind. Taking Charles Robinson with him, he went to southeast Kansas in the hopes that personal intervention would cool local tempers. Both factions received them well. The tour climaxed on June 14 with an address to a large bipartisan crowd in Fort Scott.

Denver told them he would forget all wrongs done in the past, that his mission was to secure peace for the future. He suggested that new county officials be elected and that the border be patrolled by federal troops. He asked all guerrilla organizations to disband and he promised that none of the outstanding warrants would be served until they had passed review by competent judicial tribunals.

Both sides reacted favorably to his proposals, and—despite the fact that Old Brown had returned and moved into the Fort Scott area—southeastern Kansas enjoyed an interlude of comparative peace.

After a summer of calm, John Denver, the reluctant governor, sent his resignation to President Buchanan. It was dated October 10 and had the distinction of being the first Kansas gubernatorial resignation that was not in some way either forced or requested. Denver agreed to stay at his post until his successor arrived.

The southeastern territory had grown so quiet that the governor, with the administration's agreement, removed the federal dragoons from patrol duty on November 6.

About the same time, James Montgomery was informed he had been indicted for destroying a ballot box in Mound City during the January elections. Montgomery responded characteristically—he went jayhawking.

Weary, Denver turned the territory over to Secretary of State Hugh B. Walsh, and left Kansas.

11.

KANSAS IS A STATE—AND THE NATION IS AT WAR

Walsh immediately wrote to Washington: "The notorious James Montgomery, encouraged by the support of the leading Republican press in the territory, has recommenced his system of marauding and plundering." The acting-governor requested help.

Meanwhile Montgomery and his band were pillaging and burning without restraint. Proslavery men captured a Jayhawker named Benjamin Rice—once indicted for murder but never jailed, now accused of robbery. Lacking the flair of their border-crossing compatriots, they neither hanged nor shot him, but locked him up in Fort Scott.

Old Brown considered this outrageous. The old man had been forced back to the territory in midsummer by the betrayal of a confidant. Back East he had been deep into the plans that eventually matured into his attack on Harpers Ferry when his "drillmaster," Hugh Forbes, informed on him. Brown denied the accusation vehemently and claimed the company he was organizing was bound for the Kansas Territory. Settlers, nothing more. To prove it, he promptly left for Kansas.

He behaved admirably those first few months, working in the fields as the family patriarch and visiting various Free Soil leaders. He congratulated Charles Robinson on the success of the Free Soil cause but insisted, "Nothing but war can extinguish slavery and the sooner war is inaugurated, the better."

John Brown was not a man to remain inactive long. Learning that Montgomery was planning to rescue Rice, he went to see the Jayhawker. Montgomery agreed to let him ride with the party, but only on the condition that the old man stay in the background. Brown agreed.

The raid went smoothly. Only one man was foolhardy enough to fire on the Free Soilers, and he was promptly shot through the heart. Then the Jayhawkers walked over his body and plundered his store of seven thousand dollars worth of goods.

The taste of action set Brown's appetite raving. Montgomery had had trouble keeping the old man in line. The Jayhawker said, "There wouldn't have been one stone left on another if I had let him have command."

Samuel Medary, the sixth territorial governor, arrived in Kansas on December 20, 1858. Old Brown welcomed him three days later in the best territorial tradition by leading a band across the border into Missouri and staging a night raid, stripping all goods and valuables from fifteen families, freeing eleven slaves and killing one Missourian.

The raiders rode back into the territory with the plunder and liberated slaves and set up camp at Sugar Creek, north of Fort Scott. Brown fortified his position and announced he would be taken by no one.

Governor Stewart of Missouri sent appeals to Governor

Medary and to President Buchanan. He also asked the Missouri legislature to take whatever steps they thought necessary, and gave the lawmakers testimony from thirty-five border Missourians describing outrages committed by Jayhawkers on Missouri soil.

Missouri legislators quickly introduced a bill authorizing a local military force to patrol the border. Missourians raiding Kansas was one thing, but Kansans raiding Missouri was unthinkable. The bill was referred to a committee, which returned a remarkably sensible and restrained report. The committee concluded that the depredations were the work of a few, that most Kansans were law abiding, and recommended an honest attempt at peaceful settlement before resorting to force. It pointed out that since most of the troops would be raised from border Missourians who had suffered at the Jayhawkers' hands, they were liable to act in a retaliatory manner rather than a defensive one, indeed might even launch an armed invasion against Kansas. Therefore, they advised against armed patrols and suggested that rewards be offered for the greatest offenders.

Governor Medary telegraphed Buchanan and admitted Kansas to be at fault in the border troubles. He asked the commandants of Forts Leavenworth and Riley to send military assistance, and he requested the territorial legislature to take action against Montgomery and Brown. Medary was cheered when Washington authorized a reward of $250 each for Montgomery and Brown. But the following day, inexplicably, the administration ordered federal dragoons—just called out for border duty—back to their forts.

Old Brown was not impressed by the $250 offered for

his capture. But he was impressed when Governor Stewart offered $3000 for him. Probably, too, he was growing restless sitting in his camp at Sugar Creek. Possibly his plans called for him to move along at that time anyway. Whatever the cause, he broke camp and headed toward Nebraska with his company and the liberated slaves.

Medary ordered federal troops into the field after him. It was a serious game of hounds-and-fox across the rolling plains of Kansas, but Old Brown won what territorial residents tagged "The Battle of the Spurs," crossed safely into Nebraska and conducted the ex-slaves up to Canada. Everything had gone exactly as Old Brown had hoped, and with this encouragement behind him, he turned his thoughts once again to Virginia where he hoped to inspire a mass uprising of slaves.

Montgomery made a peace offer. He would suspend all jayhawking activities if Medary would guarantee that neither Montgomery nor any of his men would be arrested for past crimes and that all Proslavery men the Jayhawkers had driven from the territory would be kept out. Medary consulted the legislature. An amnesty bill was quickly passed but the legislators, of course, could not meet his second demand. Even if they had been inclined to do so, there was no way to enforce such a guarantee.

Montgomery accepted the amnesty graciously, and took upon himself responsibility for his second condition. He did this by repeatedly raiding into Missouri. Another Jayhawker, Captain Eli Snyder, a blacksmith who had driven off Hamilton's men when they tried to round him up for the Marais des Cygnes Massacre, led a company against a Border Ruffian headquarters and burned it to the ground along with the four Missourians who were barricaded in it.

Governor Medary asked his legislature for help. It responded by voting to support him in "any legal measures to restore peace," which meant absolutely nothing.

Their duty done, the lawmakers turned back to affairs of greater interest—mainly factional, special-interest feuds behind the united Free Soil front, questions of patronage, and the passing of numerous liberal marriage and divorce laws. So progressive were these latter that one legislator with a sense of humor introduced a bill abolishing marriage altogether and establishing free love in Kansas.

But the legislature did tackle a couple of serious issues. Since the Dred Scott decision, not even free Negroes had been safe in the territory. Several attempts had been made to kidnap such men and a few of them actually were spirited across the border and sold into slavery. When a group of thirteen black freemen around Lawrence expressed apprehension, Free Soiler Dr. John Doy and his son offered to conduct them safely to Iowa where no such danger existed.

Border Ruffians overtook the party, disregarded the free papers carried by the blacks, and forced everyone across the border into Weston, Missouri. Doy and his son were jailed for slave-stealing.

The Kansas legislature now voted an appropriation of one thousand dollars for the defense of Doy and his son and authorized Medary to appoint a defense counsel.

The legislature also arranged another constitutional convention, this one to be held on July 4. And immediately before adjournment, they passed an act abolishing slavery in the territory. Governor Medary gave the bill a pocket veto—which the legislature chose to ignore. They celebrated the demise of slavery in Kansas by gathering around a great bonfire at midnight and tossing in the slavery code enacted by their predecessors.

Doy was tried in Missouri in early March. The prosecuting attorney spouted gluts of impassioned oratory and pointed out with great concern that, "If we allow our negroes to be stolen with impunity, our fair-skinned daughters will be reduced to performing the contemptible drudgery in the kitchen."

Persuasive as Missourians might have found this argument, the facts remained—Doy had been arrested illegally in Kansas and all the blacks with him possessed papers proving they were free men. The jury was hung and Dr. Doy went free. But only for two months. Then he was rearrested, tried again, and this time convicted and sentenced to five years in prison.

Free Soilers rose to the occasion, rode across the border and broke the hapless doctor from jail. They sent him by underground railroad to Canada.

Spring passed without major incident. The jayhawking period—mainly because Montgomery was in control of the southeastern territory—came to an end.

Kansas' expanding population was pressuring the available land, so President Buchanan passed a part of his summer signing new treaties with the Indians. The net result, naturally, was less land for the Indians.

On July 4, Free Soilers and Proslavery men in the southeast gathered at Fort Scott for a mutual Independence Day frolic. Long-time enemies drank and sported together, vows of friendship were exchanged and promises were made to wipe out the memories of past transgressions and to start fresh.

Up north delegates convened at Wyandotte to begin drafting yet another territorial constitution. Thirty-five of the fifty-two delegates were members of a party only a few months old in the Kansas Territory—the Republican party. The Free State party, isolated, unconnected with national parties and concerned with a local problem, had outlived its usefulness. Its goal all but achieved, it disintegrated and its disparate elements came together under the banner of Republicanism, eager to deal with slavery on a national level.

The delegates worked with enthusiasm, their harmony due in large part to the fact that few of the leaders who had been instrumental at the Topeka, Lecompton and Leavenworth draftings were present. So great was the desire of both sides to bury the past that a general amnesty covering all prosecutions springing from political differences was declared. Both Republican and Democratic delegates worked with integrity, and the constitution they wrote was a reasonable and good document. Knowing the battle for the Kansas Territory had shifted from the territory to Washington, Proslavery elements raised only a token protest against this Free State constitution. And on October 4, nearly sixteen thousand Kansans went to the polls and ratified the Wyandotte Constitution by a majority of 2-to-1.

Twelve days later, Old John Brown rocked the nation by seizing the federal armory at Harpers Ferry. Brown was trying to make his dream reality. Slaves across Virginia would take up arms and flock to him. Strongholds, independent nations of liberated blacks, would be organized in the mountains of Maryland and Virginia. Slavery was dead. And Old Brown was its executioner. But his dream ended less than forty-eight hours later when, after a short battle in which he was seriously wounded, Brown surrendered to a small force of United States Marines under the command of Colonel Robert E. Lee. Ten of his followers, including two of his sons, had been killed. Six more were captured. The remaining handful escaped.

John Brown was jailed in Charlestown, Virginia, tried and convicted of murder, slave insurrection and treason to the State of Virginia. On December 2 he was hanged. Although his plan failed completely, Old Brown's attack was a pair of spurs jammed into the nation's flanks as it raced toward civil war. Many responsible Northerners, most of them antislave themselves, denounced the act. But martyrs make better copy than murderers and Brown was rapidly canonized. Giant figures of the American scene like Ralph Waldo Emerson and Henry David Thoreau called him a saint and a hero. And in these hosannas the South found ample proof—not that it needed any more—that the North was bent on its destruction.

The day John Brown was executed, Abraham Lincoln delivered speeches in three Missouri bordertowns. The next morning he crossed into Kansas to campaign.

Christmas and New Year's Day passed without incident in the territory and a short time later the Wyandotte Constitution was introduced in Congress. On March 29, 1860, the Committee on Territories recommended that Kansas be admitted to the Union.

But recommendation and actual admission were two different things and Kansas soon found, as should have been no surprise, that she was not the most popular potential state on the North American continent. She was lost to the South. If she became a state, she would be a free state. But so long as she remained a territory, then, according to the Dred Scott decision, slavery was guaranteed there by law. The South was determined that she should not be admitted to the Union. Many Northerners, embarrassed by the excesses of Lane and Montgomery and their ilk, and knowing the explosively passionate mood of the South, were not eager to take the territory into the sisterhood of states.

Debate on the question spanned all of 1860 and penetrated into 1861. Senator James S. Green of Missouri led the southern opposition. Kansas had insufficient arable land, he claimed. It was senseless even to consider admission without first lopping off thirty thousand square acres for her from the Nebraska Territory. "Without this addition," he said, "Kansas must be weak, puerile, sickly, in debt, and at no time capable of maintaining herself." This was ridiculous, but circumstances conspired to give some semblance of credence to Green's claims. Kansas had boomed too quickly. Overexpansion now plunged the territory into a financial depression. On top of this, a severe drought struck. The parched earth cracked and seeds would not put forth the smallest of roots. Settlers left by the score. One beaten man said, "Kansas will never become a free or slave state until the rest of the world is overpopulated. Nobody who has the strength to walk, or money to pay for conveyance, will stay long."

But many did stay, determined to endure. Fifteen thousand people were thrown on public charity and aid societies sent nearly ten million pounds of food, clothing and supplies.

While Kansas burned, Washington debated. Senator Louis T. Wigfall of Texas called the Kansans outlaws and land pirates and said, "I will not consent that Texas shall associate with such a State as this would be." He spoke for the South in general.

But as rankling a thorn as Kansas had long been, and still was, the nation had something bigger on its mind—1860 was an election year.

The Republican party was only six years old, but it had already matured into a strong political force. Republicans had been highly successful in the congressional elections of 1856 and now they were stalking the Presidency. They held their May convention in Chicago and, bypassing William Seward and Salmon Chase for reasons of strategy, they nominated Abraham Lincoln on the third ballot.

The Democrats were split in two. The moderates nominated Stephen Douglas. The hardcore slavery states of the cotton belt bolted, formed the Southern Democrats and nominated John C. Breckenridge, a Proslavery extremist.

A group of genteel northern moderates formed the National Constitutional Union, which stood for the happy generalities of Constitution, Union and law enforcement. Their candidate was John Bell of Tennessee.

It was a hardfought, colorful campaign with torchlight marches, mass rallys and impassioned stump speeches. Republicans paraded with sections of rail fences on their shoulders, symbolizing Old Abe the Rail-splitter. Democrats put squads of chubby boys—"Little Giants"—on display. Southern Democrats offered minstrel shows and patriotic songs of a sectional nature. The National Constitutional Union, too gentlemanly and refined for the tastes of the people, did the best it could.

The nation soared to near fever pitch. Back in southeast Kansas—catching the spirit of things, or just wanting to keep their hand in—Jayhawkers shot two Proslavery men to death and hung a third. Explaining to a district judge Montgomery wrote:

> Russ Hinds, hung on the 12th day of November, 1860, for man stealing. He was a drunken border ruffian, worth a great deal to hang but good for nothing else. He had caught a fugitive slave, and carried him back to Missouri for sake of a reward. He was condemned by a jury of twelve men, the law being found in the 16th verse of Exodus XXI. [And he that stealeth a man, and selleth him, or if he be found in his hand, he shall sure be put to death.]

On November 6, Americans went to the polls. Douglas, although receiving a sizeable popular vote, carried only Missouri. Bell took Virginia, Kentucky and Tennessee. Lincoln carried every free state, and Breckenridge carried every cotton state, with North Carolina tagging along too. The breakdown was:

	Popular Votes	*Electoral Votes*
Lincoln	1,855,452	180
Douglas	1,376,957	12
Breckenridge	849,781	72
Bell	588,879	39

It was a decisive victory for Lincoln where it counted, the electoral college.

It also cocked the guns of the Civil War.

On December 20, 1860, South Carolina seceded from the Union.

Alabama, Florida and Mississippi followed her almost immediately. The North was in complete control of what remained of Congress, and Kansas Territory became a state on January 29. But in the rush of secession that fact seemed unimportant—to everyone but Kansans, who celebrated their new statehood lustily.

Louisiana, Georgia and Texas seceded. Delegates from the seven maverick states met in Montgomery, Alabama, on February 8 and formed the Confederate States of America, soon to be joined by Arkansas, Tennessee, Virginia and North Carolina. Panicked, Congress sent to outgoing President Buchanan a proposed Thirteenth Amendment that was designed to establish slavery in the United States as a permanent and inviolate institution.

Death threats were made against Lincoln. As the President-elect closed out his affairs in Springfield, Illinois, James H. Lane offered to furnish him a bodyguard of frontier Kansans armed with Sharps rifles and Bowie knives to see him safely to Washington.

It was a time of histrionic gesture.

Lincoln was inaugurated on March 4. He moved and spoke cautiously, standing firm against secession but trying to coax back the bolting states rather than threaten them with force and attempting to keep the vacillating border states—Maryland, Kentucky, Missouri and the area that was to become West Virginia—from throwing in with the Confederacy.

It was no use.

On the morning of April 12, 1861, bleeding Kansas had been a state for two and a half months.

On the morning of April 12, 1861, Confederate batteries opened fire on Fort Sumter, and the nation, having played its prelude in the Kansas Territory, sounded the full, opening strains of the most brutal symphony in its history, the Civil War.

EPILOGUE

The conflict in the Kansas Territory was of cataclysmic importance to the United States of the nineteenth century. The North and the South had grown quite apart by 1850, and passage of the Kansas-Nebraska Act along with the implementation of the doctrine of popular sovereignty laid the territory before the divided nation as a prize to be taken by the stronger side. It was an open invitation to battle, and the implication was clear to both factions: the victor would no doubt determine the future of slavery in the United States for at least the next decade, and quite possibly for all times. The Kansas Territory polarized both sides and made impossible whatever slight chance of reconciliation might have existed. The first gunfire crackled along the Kansas-Missouri border in 1854, and the war that began there did not end until General Robert E. Lee surrendered to General Ulysses S. Grant at Appomattox on April 9, 1865. (Some small Confederate units fought on for another month, but the actual conclusion of the war occurred at Appomattox.)

Kansas contributed heavily to the Union army, supplying the North with twenty thousand of her less than thirty thousand eligible men. She was the scene of guerrilla warfare throughout the conflict, and gave rise to the Kansas Redlegs, a paramilitary band of robbers and murderers who killed and burned out southern sympathizers in Missouri. In turn, she soaked up the blood of her own citizens when Missouri Bush Rangers raided across her border. The most infamous of these was William C. Quantrill, who led his men against Lawrence on August 21, 1863, burned the town to the ground and murdered more than one hundred and fifty civilians. Several formal military engagements were fought in Kansas. The largest was the Battle of Mine Creek in which Confederate General Sterling Price, having taken a beating at Westport several days earlier, was given a *coup de grâce*—a defeat that ended Confederate hopes of controlling the West. Eleven years followed the signing of the Kansas-Nebraska Act before Kansas, the thirty-fourth state, put aside her arms, laid down to rest and began the slow process of healing herself.

On a larger scale, the wars in Kansas were no more than another stone set upon an edifice that is still, even to this day, unfinished. Though certainly of greater influence than preceding stones, Kansas did not determine, nor did the Civil War itself, the shape of the final structure. That is still unknown to us, and will perhaps remain so until the children of our children's children are born. The relationship between whites and blacks, and between whites and other whites who view the issue with opposing attitudes, has always been uneasy in this country at the best mo-

ments, ferocious and bloody at the worst. It is of fundamental importance to be familiar with and to understand
our past. If we do not, we risk the great danger of becoming its victims, of acting in passionate ignorance and
repeating our mistakes in ever increasing proportions.
And the lives that were lost in Kansas, and the horror of
the Civil War, will have been without any purpose at all
and may well pale in the face of some greater horror that
lies waiting for us in the future.

BIBLIOGRAPHY

BOOKS

Bailes, K. E. *Rider on the Wind: Jim Lane and Kansas.*
Shawnee Mission, Kansas, 1962.

Brewerbon, G. D. *The War in Kansas.* New York, 1856.

Brown, G. W. *The Rescue of Kansas from Slavery.* Rockford,
Illinois, 1902.

Carroll, C. *The Negro a Beast* or *In the Image of God.* St.
Louis, Missouri, 1900.

Connely, W. E. *History of Kansas.* Vols. I, II. Chicago, 1928.

————. *John Brown.* Topeka, 1900.

————. *Kansas Territorial Governors.* Topeka, 1900.

Cook, J. R. *The Border and the Buffalo.* Chicago, 1938.

Eldridge, S. W. *Recollections of Early Days in Kansas.*
Topeka, 1920.

Filler, L. *The Crusade Against Slavery.* New York, 1960.

Hinton, R. J. *John Brown and His Men.* New York, 1904.

Howe, C. C. *This Place Called Konsar.* Norman, Oklahoma,
1952.

Johnson, S. A. *The Battle Cry of Freedom.* Lawrence, 1954.

Merrill, O. N. *A True History of the Kansas Wars.* New
York, 1932.

Monaghan, J. *Civil War on the Western Border, 1854–1865.* Boston, 1955.

Morison, S. E. *The Oxford History of the American People.* New York, 1965.

Nichols, A. *Bleeding Kansas.* New York, 1954.

Pratt, F. *Ordeal by Fire.* New York, 1948.

Rhodes, J. F. *History of the United States from the Compromise of 1850.* Vols. I, II. New York, 1928.

Spring, L. W. *Kansas: The Prelude to the War for the Union.* Boston and New York, 1892.

Stephenson, W. H. *The Political Career of General James H. Lane.* Topeka, 1930.

Stevens, W. B. *Missouri the Center State, 1821–1915.* St. Louis, 1915.

Street, J. *The Civil War.* New York, 1953.

Zornow, W. F. *Kansas.* Norman, Oklahoma, 1957.

ARTICLES

Bridgman, E. P. "Bleeding Kansas and the Pottawattomi Murders." *Mississippi Valley Historical Review,* March 1920.

Carruth, W. H. "New England in Kansas." *New England Magazine,* March 1897.

Chandler, C. L. "Two Letters from Kansas, 1855–1856." *Mississippi Valley Historical Review,* June 1942.

Davis, G. D. "Arkansas and the Blood of Kansas." *Journal of Southern History,* November 1950.

Hodder, F. H. "Railroad Background of the Kansas-Nebraska Bill." *Mississippi Valley Historical Review,* June 1925.

Johannsen, R. W. "Kansas-Nebraska Act and the Pacific Northwest." *Pacific Historical Review,* May 1953.

Klem, M. J. "Missouri in the Kansas Struggle." *Mississippi Valley Historical Society Proceedings,* Vol. IX, Part III.

Lynch, W. O. "Popular Sovereignty and the Colonization of Kansas from 1854 to 1860." *Mississippi Valley Historical Society Proceedings,* Vol. IX, Part III.

Malin, J. C. "Colonel Harvey and His Forty Thieves." *Mississippi Valley Historical Review,* June 1932.

————. "Judge Lecompte and the 'Sack of Lawrence,' May 21, 1856." (Part One: The Contemporary Phase.) *Kansas Historical Quarterly,* August 1953.

————. "Judge Lecompte and the 'Sack of Lawrence,' May 21, 1856." (Part Two: The Historical Phase.) *Kansas Historical Quarterly,* November 1953.

————. "Pro-slavery Background of the Kansas Struggle." *Mississippi Valley Historical Review,* December 1923.

Nichols, R. F. "Kansas-Nebraska Act: A Century of Historiography." *Mississippi Valley Historical Review,* September 1956.

Parks, J. H. "Tennessee Whigs and the Kansas-Nebraska Bill." *Journal of Southern History,* August 1944.

Reznikoff, C. "Scenes and Characters from the American Epic; Bleeding Kansas, 1856." *Menorah Journal,* January 1947.

Russel, R. R. "Issues in the Congressional Struggle Over the Kansas-Nebraska Bill, 1854." *Journal of Southern History,* May 1963.

Viles, J. "Sections and Sectionalism in a Border State." *Mississippi Valley Historical Review,* June 1934.

INDEX